The FOCALGUIDE to Weddings and Special Occasions

THE (f) FOCALGUIDES TO

	Basic Photography
COLOUR	David Lynch
EFFECTS AND TRICKS	Günter Spitzing
EXPOSURE	David Lynch
LIGHTING	Paul Petzold
LOW LIGHT PHOTOGRAPHY	Paul Petzold
SELLING YOUR PHOTOGRAPHS	Ed Buziak
SLIDES	Graham Saxby
	Equipment
CAMERA ACCESSORIES	Leonard Gaunt
CAMERAS	Clyde Reynolds
FILTERS	Clyde Reynolds
FLASH	Günter Spitzing
LARGER FORMAT CAMERAS	Sidney Ray
LENSES	Leonard Gaunt
SLIDE-TAPE	Brian Duncalf
35 mm	Leonard Gaunt
THE 35 mm SINGLE-LENS REFLEX	Leonard Gaunt
	Processing
CIBACHROME	Jack H. Coote
COLOUR FILM PROCESSING	Derek Watkins
COLOUR PRINTING	Jack H. Coote
THE DARKROOM	Leonard Gaunt
ENLARGING	Günter Spitzing
HOME PROCESSING	Ralph Jacobson
	Subjects
ACTION PHOTOGRAPHY	Don Morley
BIRD PHOTOGRAPHY	Michael W. Richards
CLOSE-UPS	Sidney Ray
MOUNTAINS	Douglas Milner
PHOTOGRAPHING PEOPLE	Alison Trapmore
PHOTOGRAPHING PLACES	D. H. Day
PLANTS AND FLOWERS	David Walton
PORTRAITS	Günter Spitzing
WEDDINGS AND SPECIAL OCCASIONS	Bob Bluffield
	Movie
MOVIEMAKING	Paul Petzold
SHOOTING ANIMATION	Zoran Perisic

The FOCALGUIDE to Weddings and Special Occasions

Bob Bluffield

Focal Press · London

Focal/Hastings House · New York

BL British Library Cataloguing in Publication Data

Bluffield, Bob
The focalguide to weddings and special occasions.
1. Wedding photography 2. Photography
I. Title
778.9′9′3925 TR575

ISBN (excl. USA) 0 240 51000 3
ISBN (USA only) 0 8038 2380 0

I dedicate this book to Ron Hayward of Wilkin Studios, Enfield, who is largely responsible for the shaping of my professional career. Without his help and guidance I may never have started in wedding and social photography.

Text set in 10/12 pt Photon Univers, printed and bound in Great Britain at The Pitman Press, Bath

Contents

Introduction

Several years ago, when I first started taking wedding photographs as a weekend operator, I was astonished at the lack of instructional books dealing with the subject of social photography. After a considerable search around specialist book shops I eventually found a couple of rather dated USA publications. Neither of these gave me any inspiration and I had to learn by studying the work of experienced wedding photographers and fashion photography in the quality bridal magazines.

It seems strange that there is an abundance of books on almost every other aspect of photography yet so few writers have bothered to explain the 'secrets' of photographing weddings. A few books have appeared recently but even these neglect to instruct those wishing to make a start as social photographers. There is obviously a need for a book catering for the advanced amateur and semi-professional photographer. Hopefully this book fills this need.

Social photography, more especially wedding coverage, depends heavily on the help of part-timers. Yet, comparatively few professional photographers are willing to give well-defined coaching to newcomers. Social photography was not respected as a profession until a decade ago largely because of the attitude of those in the profession itself. A growing public awareness about photography and the dramatic interest taken by the professional representative bodies, such as the Professional Photographers' Association (USA) and the Institute of Incorporated Photographers (UK) have led to a new breed of more capable social photographers. Yet, few have been interested in the efforts of amateur or semi-professional photographers.

Having joined the professional ranks myself from a lowly training as a Saturday wedding operator, I can appreciate the points of view of both professional and amateur. Firstly, I recognize the vast and untapped talent that *could* be recruited from the amateur ranks, but I also appreciate the professional view that inexperienced amateurs passing themselves off as social photographers can cause damage to the profession.

First and foremost, I must emphasize that I subscribe firmly to the belief that an untrained person should not, on any count, accept a photographic assignment as important as a wedding. However, there is no formal programme for training photographers to cover a social event such as a wedding. The only way to get into the business is by finding a studio willing to train you, or to teach yourself. Either way can be hard work and the latter is not recommended unless you have acquired some knowledge as to how a professional studio operates. This book has been published to try and bridge the gap by giving sufficient knowledge to advanced amateurs to enable them to join a professional studio without the necessity for extensive training. It is not intended to *replace* training, but to aid it.

I am aware that the instruction I offer in this book may upset a few of my fellow professionals because they feel that amateurs should be positively *discouraged* from becoming social photographers. However, most agree that standards must continue to improve and that new creative talent is constantly required to provide a steady and healthy growth within the business.

Social photographic coverage is no longer intended to be stiff and starchy. Casual, journalistic forms of coverage are standard practice on both sides of the Atlantic. Photographers are having to adapt to changing styles in all areas of the art; social photography is no exception. I have attempted to describe these styles of coverage throughout the text and accompanying illustrations. The public are also more aware of variations in style between different photographers and for this reason you will need to develop your own original style. This can be achieved in several ways; by adopting your own methods of posing, by using a range of special effects and equipment to obtain a new 'angle' or by creating your own multi-image compositions. Each is mentioned, albeit briefly in the text, but the purpose is not so much to hand you stereotyped information that can be copied but more to provide 'food for thought' so that you can develop your own individualistic form of coverage no matter what the occasion.

Weddings and other social occasions have basic similarities in whichever country they take place. However, there are certain variations of tradition and attitudes among different nationalities which will affect the photographer. For example, in the USA much greater importance is attached to the role of the photographer than in the UK. It is quite normal for a couple and their main wedding guests (parents, bridesmaids, ushers, etc.) to dress formally prior to the wedding and to go to the photographer's studio where the groups and 'official' bridal portraits will be shot in advance. Similarly, even when a couple are marrying in church, the bride will often see the groom on the wedding day before she reaches the altar. Yet, in the UK, this is still widely considered to be very unlucky. One of the main differences between weddings in the UK and the USA is the home ceremony. In the UK it is not possible to marry in one's own home; whereas, in the USA, the entire ceremony and reception can be held at the bride's home.

I have already mentioned that in the USA photography is viewed with greater importance than in the UK. This extends to the freedom of operation that their photographers are allowed; freedom to choose beautiful natural settings where they can photograph the bridal couple to the best advantage. As a consequence, several wedding photographers in the USA have become internationally well-known.

Finally, I have tried in this book to give a basic guide to the principles of wedding photography, including both the formal and the more imaginative approaches. Although the majority of the book is written around the theme of the Western church wedding, the basic techniques described are intended to be adaptable to a variety of social occasions.

Wedding Photography

Despite figures which show that the percentage of people who get married is on the decrease, there is nothing to suggest an end to the 'institution' of marriage as we know it. People are basically old fashioned and although there is a wider acceptance of less formal arrangements, many of these eventually turn to marriage.
Weddings have become, over the years, big business for any company involved in providing services or products necessary to comply with the traditions. Caterers, chauffeur-driven car hire firms, photographers, dressmakers and numerous others owe a substantial part of their trade to weddings.

Photographers

Professional photographic coverage at weddings has changed dramatically over recent years. The more progressive workers take the casual approach pioneered in America by such eminent wedding masters as Jack Curtis, Rocky Gunn and Bill Stockwell.
Wedding photography has become much more lively. Brighter portrayal, brought about by the introduction of machine-made colour prints and the increasing use of creative skills to capture mood, has lifted the wedding photographer into a position of respect.
It is encouraging to see the changes that have already taken place in wedding photography but there remains plenty of room for further improvements. The older-style photographers, those with more business acumen than talent, are gradually being replaced by more creative photographers.
Unfortunately, the situation once existed where owning a camera was all it took to earn a 'fast buck' taking wedding photographs. Many of these 'photographers' were little more than snapshooters but they nevertheless found a niche and remained. Lack of competi-

tion gave them a sense of security until such time as newcomers arrived to put up a challenge. Today ability plays a much greater role. If you are able to express your creativity in a lively and imaginative way you will find opportunities for success even though the competition can be fierce.
Weddings are covered chiefly by the 'general practitioners' many of whom have devoted the major part of their businesses towards weddings and portraiture. They have become the mainstay of wedding practice and as such are often regarded as the specialists.

Part-timers

A large number of wedding photographers operate semi-professionally, chiefly from their own homes. Weddings, because they usually occur on Saturdays, allow such photographers the benefit of working in another occupation. Frequently 'amateurs' fit the bill and it is here that vast opportunity does exist. You can either work for yourself or freelance your services to others already established in the wedding business. Many studios welcome extra help particularly during the busy summer months when their available personnel may be stretched.
There are a number of firms specializing in nothing but weddings, though they are considerably outnumbered by individual and GP photographers. These firms usually work from a central base but may draw their trade from a large area by employing the services of agents and representatives. Their standards of coverage obviously vary with the photographer handling the job.
A handful of newspapers, usually those in rural areas, also provide an occasional wedding photography service operated by their own staff. There is unlikely to be any scope here for the beginner or anyone from outside the immediate employ of the newspaper.

The professional's role

The professional photographer is expected to turn up on time and take a series of photographs that depict the character and mood of the wedding. Most succeed in providing this service albeit with varying degrees of ability and finesse.

Couples choose a professional photographer because they expect him to be sufficiently expert about his subject and capable of producing the best record of the occasion. Couples can choose unwisely and they may book the first photographer they come across taking little account of his proficiency. Although few would openly admit it, some couples are disappointed with their photographs. Had they shopped around then the chances are that they could have engaged a better photographer.

The public are growing more aware of photography. The differences between good and shoddy work are being recognized, however wedding photographs are seldom rejected if they are bad purely because there is never the chance to shoot them again. In other areas of commercial photography such as advertising, poor quality is given far stricter treatment and bad workers have less chance of survival. Yet, despite this criticism, rapid improvements have been made in wedding photography and today the customer receives a far better deal than ever before.

The professional wedding photographer accepts that he must operate under a good many pressures, most unique to the nature of the job. It matters very little to the couple whether or not it is raining. They still, quite rightly, expect a good set of photographs despite the weather conditions or any other problems that may prevail.

Wedding guests are sometimes difficult to handle. They may not wish to be coaxed into a position in a group. Others may get in the official photographer's way with their own cameras. To cope with this and other problems the wedding photographer must learn to be flexible, capable of adapting to a variety of situations. If he gets ruffled or annoyed then it means that he has accepted defeat!

The majority of weddings pass smoothly with everyone willing to lend a helping hand if asked. However, you must be warned to expect a few that are less easy to handle during some period in your career.

Wedding photographers, within the confines of a short period, work harder than photographers handling other types of work. The wedding operator must possess vast stamina, a good sense of humour, a placid temperament and be 100% enthusiastic about his work. If you have all of these ingredients coupled with sufficient photographic knowledge, then you will probably make a very good wedding photographer.

Recording the event

Often, whatever his own views on photography, a wedding photographer has to go through the customary formalized ritual. You must take the same series of stereotyped pictures because this is what your customers expect. With a little care though, you can add a great deal of life and sparkle to even the most standard package.

Some professionals are hostile towards anyone carrying a camera who appears at the church. On the other hand, many professionals try to assist any guests who have their cameras with them. In return they generally find that they receive cooperation and can therefore carry out their work unhindered.

One of the main points of this book is to try and guide amateurs in the right direction. In so doing, a better understanding can be established between professional and amateur photographers at a wedding.

The amateur's role

The professional attends weddings purely for commercial reasons. In reverse the amateur is there as a guest of the couple, invited to join them in their celebrations of the happy occasion. If he takes along his camera and is able to take some interesting photographs then this is a bonus. Frequently amateurs forget this. Instead they overindulge in their hobby and duplicate *every* photograph that the professional has set up.

This proves to be an exercise of little value (unless disaster should strike the professional) and this unnecessary copying holds up proceedings. The professional is then left to 'carry the can' for taking too much time.

The amateur has a wealth of opportunity about him at a wedding just waiting to be exploited while the professional is engaged with the official record.

Later sections describe both ways of covering a wedding: (a) the official record and (b) the candid approach. The first is of most interest to any serious reader who is keen to become a professional or semi-professional wedding photographer. The latter section is aimed predominantly at the amateur, advanced or otherwise, who takes along his camera purely for his own enjoyment. Although there can be a certain overlap on the two methods, the professional's role seldom allows him the opportunity to look for many candid shots.

Straightforward record photography

For some strange reason the largest guest orders come from those that have taken their own cameras to the wedding. It is usually the same people that have duplicated the photographs taken by the professional. When asked the reason they are buying the same pictures that they themselves have taken, the answer is always the same: 'I want to cover myself in case my pictures do not come out'. Most people that take their own cameras along to a wedding want no more than a simple record of the event. If snapshots are all that matter then obviously the simplest method of obtaining such photographs is to stay *behind* the professional and copy the compositions he sets up.

This book does not cover the basic techniques of camera operation. So, if you are unsure then pick up your camera instruction book and learn exactly what the various controls are for. The *Focalguide to Cameras* is one book that provides a great deal of basic information and is strongly recommended. Even if you know exactly how your camera operates, and understand its full potential, it is still possible to go wrong in the heat of the moment. One of the most common mistakes is to over- or underexpose to a degree that the negative becomes unprintable. First and foremost, ensure that the correct ASA rating for the film you are using is set on the dial of your camera meter (if it has a built in exposure meter) or separate light meter.

The next commonplace fault is in focusing. Be careful and critical. On most cameras the problems of focusing are fairly simple. On SLRs you will see your subject through the lens and you should therefore be able to focus quickly and accurately. Similarly, cameras with split-image focusing are simple to operate. Recent developments have introduced cameras that focus themselves and these are naturally very convenient.

There are occasions, such as in poor light, when you may not be certain of your focusing. In these circumstances you can judge the distance between camera and subject, and set the distance scale of the lens appropriately. A small lens opening (large *f*-number) can also be used to give a larger depth of field, which is shown on the depth of field of the lens. This gives you the areas which are in focus for a particular aperture depending on what distance the lens has been set for. An example of this might be a 50 mm lens set at an aperture of *f*11. If the distance scale on this lens has been set at 3 m (10 ft), the depth of field scale would show that anything between 1.5 m (5 ft) and infinity would be recorded in focus on your film. However, if a wider aperture is used at the same distance, the depth of focus is much less. Thus at *f*4 your focusing needs to be more accurate because your depth of field now lies between 2.5 m (8 ft) and 4 m (13 ft), anything nearer or further from the camera is out of focus. Depth of field used in this way can act as compensation at times when you are unsure of your focus, but it must be remembered that the selection of a small aperture results in the need to use a slower shutter speed to obtain correct exposure. This may become an overruling factor in poor light when a wide aperture may be used to allow you to safely 'hand-hold' the camera.

Composing the picture

Unless you are doing your own printing or are using a laboratory that will be making selective enlargements from a part of the negative (expensive when printing colour), be sure to fill your frame when composing your photograph. If you are using a standard lens on your camera (40 mm to 55 mm with most 35 mm cameras, 75 or 80 mm with most 6 × 6 cm cameras) you will probably find that by standing next to or slightly behind the official photographer you will have a similar viewpoint. The majority of wedding photographs taken by a professional are shot using a standard lens. If he uses a roll film camera (6 × 6 cm on 120 film) as most do, then your 35 mm camera fitted with standard lens will have roughly the same area in the viewfinder. The difference being that a 35 mm camera produces an oblong image, whereas a 6 × 6 cm format produces a square image.

Traditional photographs

The professional photographer's work revolves chiefly around the traditional rigidly posed groups and full-length, three-quarter and close-up studies of the bride and groom. If they had the opportunity and were not governed so tightly by the economics of professional wedding coverage, the chances are that many professionals would opt for taking more creative photographs. However the traditional standard poses sell the most and similarly these are chosen by most snapshooters.

Record photography means exactly that – a record of the events. For his own immediate record there is little need for the basic photographer to look beyond what the professional is covering.

To produce a suitable selection try including a couple of the family groups, perhaps a full-length of the parents, full-length and head-and-shoulders studies of the couple as well as one of each of them on their own and a picture of them departing in their car.

Most professional photographers cover a wedding in a methodical way. It is normal to begin the post-ceremony photography by taking shots of the couple together. Gradually the groups are built up from small to large. By watching the professional's routine you will soon know when to click your shutter. Never try to rush the professional's working methods by insisting on taking a close-up when he is working on arranging a group. This may sound like commonsense but the number who may do this is astonishing.

Getting the most from a wedding

If you have an 'eye' for an interesting photograph and want to escape from routine then a wedding can provide the ideal opportunity. The best way for an amateur to look at a wedding is in a highly personal way. You should try to produce a series of pictures that are your own interpretation of the occasion. A 'customized' set of photographs can be a pleasing additional touch to the couple's official album. An alert mind is necessary when seeking these less traditional photographs but it is difficult to describe just what to look for because the majority of such photographs happen spontaneously.

One of the advantages of covering a wedding in your own way is that it reflects *your* ideas regarding composition, viewpoint and humour. While you are actively engaged in looking for opportune moments you will also be keeping well clear of the professional's activities. For example, while the official photographer arranges a group, it can be very humorous to stand back and aim your lens at the antics of the professional as he attempts to induce some sort of order into his arrangement. The professional rarely gets the chance to see such pictures of himself in action but of the few that are taken, some of them are very humorous indeed.

The guests also present good subjects if you are adept at taking candid studies. Conversations between groups of people usually guarantee some wonderful expressions and weddings are the ideal place to look for this sort of material. A telephoto lens of medium length (105 mm or 135 mm) is useful on a SLR camera to lessen the risk of being observed while you are doing your work. Candid photographs are frequently ruined if the subjects notice the camera because people tend to pose when they know that they are being photographed. If you are not afraid to get in close then try using a wide-angle (28 mm for ultra-wide or 35 mm). Wide-angles give a tremendous depth of field at all apertures and the feeling of being 'within' the action, because of the close viewpoint, can capture the atmosphere of the occasion.

When attempting candid photographs you can learn a great deal by studing some of the fine work produced by the master French photographer, Henri Cartier-Bresson. Well known for his portrayals of people in unguarded moments, Cartier-Bresson became a specialist at what he called the 'decisive moment'. By this he came to anticipate the ultimate moment to press the shutter. A close inspection of his work will reveal something about this style of candid work and how it could be applied to wedding photography.

A further way to indulge in the candid study of weddings is to arrive early. In this way you may have the chance of taking a couple of quick arrival photographs of people approaching the ceremony or, better still, you may catch the groom and his best man taking a stiff drink in a local bar. Take care not to offend the bar landlord by taking photographs on his premises without his permission. It will be readily granted in most cases providing you ask beforehand.

Children are always wonderful subjects for the camera and you should concentrate some of your time looking for the best moments. Children become bored very quickly especially at weddings and they are likely to get up to all types of mischief. In addition to a series of candid studies you should try a few informal portraits of each child.

A good 35 mm SLR camera is an ideal tool for venturing into the offbeat study of weddings. With care you could build an album taken 'behind the scenes' of the occasion as it were. This would most certainly provide an excellent addition to the official set of pictures.

A quick eye and a fast shutter speed (1/125 second should be adequate) are necessary when you are photographing children who always change their moods and expressions very quickly. For adults you will be able to get away with slightly slower speeds. Be ready to focus rapidly or pre-focus to a set distance. A pre-focused lens could save you missing a very important shot.

On a more intimate note you may also like to look for moments that capture some of the hidden tenderness seldom included in the official record. The bride's mother shedding a few tears is one example that comes to mind. If care is not taken this shot can completely lose its meaning so take extra care to work quickly and without intrusion.

Weddings involve all kinds of emotion. Love, gentleness, gaiety, sentiment and the precious feelings that can be expressed by one person to another. The official photographer will be trying to express these moments as they affect the bride and bridegroom. You can look for these same moments as they affect others around the couple. For example, the warmth between two relatives as they meet after a long separation. As a wedding photographer you will, in time, learn to adapt to these situations.

Amateur versus professional

Most professional photographers only wish that they had the time to swap places with the amateur so that they could pursue the candid approach to wedding photography. However, commercial reasoning prevents them from doing so. If you begin working as an official operator, either full-time or semi-professionally, your professional involvement often limits the type of photographs you can take.

Primarily, all people with cameras are *photographers.* Good, bad, or indifferent, the dividing line between professional and amateur is very slim. There are good and bad professionals and good and bad amateurs. What matters most of all is the personal involvement you have with the work you are doing. The only real distinction is that one person sets out to earn money with his camera while the other does not expect any financial gain. In between is a group that is frequently forgotten; the semi-professionals.

Social photography thrives on semi-professionals and it saddens me that so many of the representative bodies of photography fail to acknowledge this fact. But in reality many professional studios would fail to function if it were not for the outside help readily given by semi-professionals.

The situation is growing easier. A large number of full-time photographers realize that sound futures can only be ensured by introducing new talent to the business. Many therefore extend a welcoming hand to new faces providing they show signs of sincere interest and are willing to learn from the bottom. A few professionals continue to keep the amateur on the other side of the fence by adopting a 'them and us' frame of mind. However, thankfully, attitudes are changing and the distinction between professional and amateur is slowly diminishing and one day a photographer's ability will be judged by the work he produces and not by the external involvements he may have.

Technique and Equipment

Numerous photographic books contain countless pages of discussion about the various makes of photographic hardwear and it is sufficient here to say just a little about equipment prior to taking you through the stages of wedding coverage.
Below is a check list of essential items you will need if you intend serious coverage of special occasions.

Checklist

1 Camera (preferably 6 × 6 cm, 6 × 4.5 cm or 6 × 7 cm) with a good quality lens. This should be thoroughly tested before packing.
2 Spare camera (perhaps a 35 mm) as a back-up should the main camera fail.
3 Light meter.
4 Electronic flash (preferably computerized) of sufficient power for many exposures.
5 Spare fully-charged batteries for your flash gun.
6 Spare electronic flash (small hand gun) as stand-by in case of failure of main gun.
7 Adequate supply of film.
8 Flash synchronization leads.
9 Spare flash synchronization leads which connect camera to flash and flash power pack to flash head when applicable. Leads have the habit of breaking on important assignments.
10 Lens hood and filters for special effects.
11 Firm tripod.
12 Spare lenses of varying focal lengths (not essential but helpful).
13 Cable release to allow tremble-free camera operation during slow shutter speeds.

14 Camera neck strap if you intend using the camera hand held.
15 Adhesive tape for sealing roll film ends (tape is sometimes missing from film ends) or for mending things temporarily.
16 Pins or weights which can be useful for holding down bride's dress train in windy weather.
17 Strong and easy-to-carry gadget bag.

The above list is comprehensive and covers most eventualities. As your involvement continues you will probably add other items you find useful.

Cameras

In the UK most official wedding photography is done on roll-film cameras usually taking negatives which are 6 × 6 cm ($2\frac{1}{4} \times 2\frac{1}{4}$ in). In recent years there have been certain changes, chiefly for economy, and other roll-film formats have been more widely accepted. Thus roll-film cameras producing negatives of 6 × 4.5 cm and 6 × 7 cm are commonly in use.

The 35 mm camera is used less by professional wedding operators in the UK than it is elsewhere. In the UK wedding coverage is based on a small compact series of photographs. Elsewhere it is not uncommon to find that well over one hundred photographs are taken and therefore 35 mm may prove to be the ideal format for economic reasons. The same also applies in the UK when photographers are requested to cover more of the occasion than they consider normal. The main shots may be taken on roll film but less informal pictures may be recorded on 35 mm.

If you intend to shoot weddings and other special occasions for profit you should check with the studio which employs you, or with the laboratory producing your prints, to see which format is favoured.

There are good and bad points about any make or type of camera. Personal preference and financial considerations obviously play a major part in this choice. When buying a camera there are various factors which need to be considered. If flash is required at all shutter speeds (highly desirable for the wedding operator) then you need to buy a camera that has a leaf shutter. These tend to be more expen-

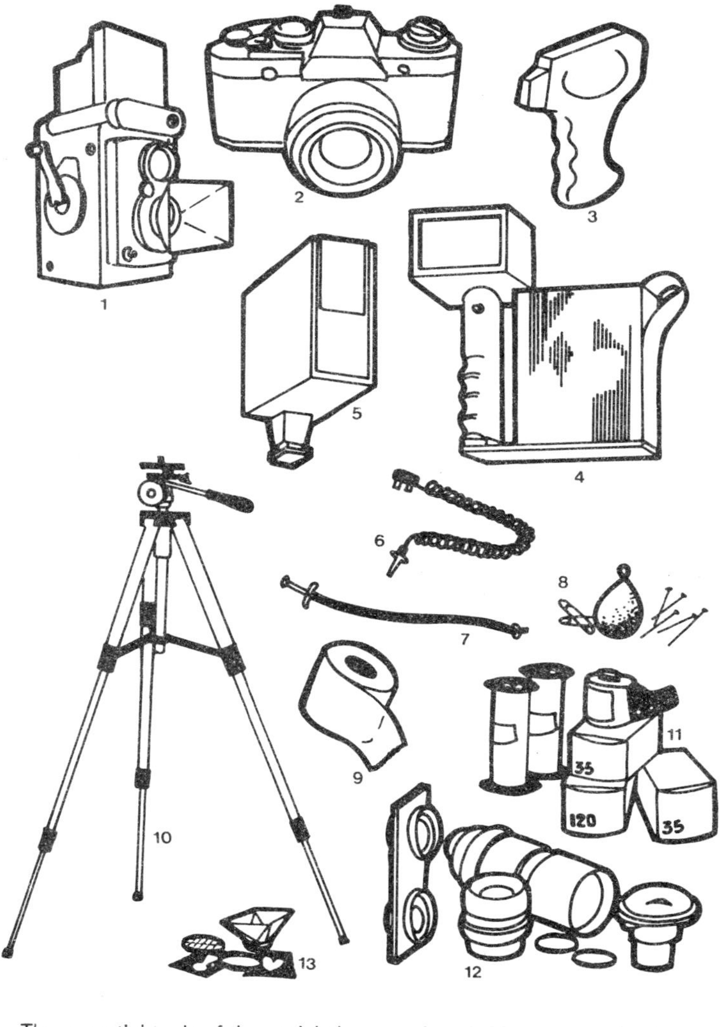

The essential tools of the social photographer. 1. Main camera (preferably 120); 2. Back-up camera (120 or 35 mm); 3. Pistol grip; 4. Reliable fast-recycling electronic flash; 5. Back-up flash gun; 6. Flash sync leads (two); 7. Cable release; 8. Pins and weights to be used on windy days; 9. Adhesive tape; 10. Tripod; 11. Adequate film supply; 12. Extra lenses as required; 13. Lens hood(s) and special effects filters.

sive than cameras with focal plane shutters but synchronization at all speeds is possible. Focal plane shutters have the disadvantage of synchronizing only at speeds of 1/125 second or slower. You also need to decide the importance of interchangeable lens facilities. Some twin-lens cameras do not have this facility yet nevertheless prove adequate for covering professional wedding assignments.

Most modern cameras are suitably constructed to withstand the rigors of professional use. Similarly, they are usually equipped with lenses of good optical quality capable of giving an acceptable degree of sharpness on even the largest prints.

The feel, weight and balance of a camera and its ease of use are aspects that will determine your ultimate choice. Read the publicity hand-outs for each camera and the reviews for any equipment that may interest you. Lastly, go and see a knowledgeable dealer and scrutinize the various cameras available.

As films become technically better with less grain on enlargements then the 35 mm format will gain in popularity with those engaged in professional social photography.

However, the introduction of SLR roll-film cameras and cameras producing negatives other than 6 × 6 cm ($2\frac{1}{4} \times 2\frac{1}{4}$ in) from a roll film, means that the larger format will continue to be the accepted norm.

SLR cameras have always been popular. The main advantage is that they allow you to gauge your composition precisely. Parallax can be a problem with rangefinder, viewfinder and twin-lens cameras when you are close focusing on a subject. Certain cameras make provisions to overcome this problem, others do not.

Flash equipment

Today the flash-bulb as such has largely been superseded by electronic flash providing fast recycling times and economy. However, the compact ranges of cameras still use bulbs, in the form of flash cubes, but these are quite costly in comparison to electronic flash. Electronic flashguns can be purchased for the price of a few rolls of film and are operated either by battery or directly from the mains. As with most things, you get what you pay for. There is little point in buying a cheap basic battery-operated gun and expecting it to work miracles. Cheap guns provide a reasonable output for normal photography of people and therefore can adequately be used by the amateur for covering some social occasions such as parties.

Beyond that, greater involvement demands more sophisticated equipment and a wide range of 'computerized' guns are on the market at varying prices, depending on output and facilities provided. The 'computerized' guns have light-sensitive sensors for cutting off the light on the gun itself when the subject has been adequately illuminated. Some have detachable sensors for placing on the camera for more precise results with bounced or angled flash.

The more sophisticated flashguns have a range of outputs. They allow you to select the lens aperture you want rather than be restricted to the setting dictated by the flashgun's light output, as is the case with manual flash or simple 'computer' models. If you are using a manual flashgun then you can find the required aperture by dividing the guide number by the distance; most flashguns have a built-in calculator to do just this. For example, if the flash has a guide number of 33 (for your film) and you are shooting a subject 3 m (10 ft) away you need to set your lens at *f*11 for correct results.

Electronic flashguns which can be recharged from the mains operate off either nickel-cadmium or wet cell accumulators. The wet cells need to be topped-up with distilled water from time to time when the levels get low. The battery normally contains little coloured balls that float when the charge is high. When the power is used up the balls drop to the bottom of their cells and this indicates that the gun needs mains-charging. Nickel-cadmium batteries last longer but they do not have the visual check on remaining power between charges as you have with the wet cell type. However, with all guns, a slowing down of the recycling time between flashes indicates that recharging is ncecessary.

Use of flash

A strong reliable gun with plenty of power is demanded by wedding and social photography, and computer-type guns are widely used for speed and performance.

Flash is not only required for illuminating your subjects in darkened interiors but it is also an ally in unsuitable outside lighting. They are used for 'fill-in' when shadows are strong and as a main light source on winter weddings.

Indoors, aim to flash from a ceiling or wall whenever possible. This gives a softer appearance and dispenses with the hard shadows characteristic of direct flash. But you must be careful not to bounce flash off coloured walls – the resulting photographs will have the same colour cast.

Occasionally flash can be used to 'lift' shots lit mainly by available light indoors. For example, when working on an aperture of *f*8 in a window area, you can lighten some of the shadows by bouncing some light at a level which would require *f*4 or *f*5.6 for full exposure – the automatic gun is simply set to *f*4 or *f*5.6.

'Red eyes' on direct flashlit shots are one of the failings of a good many amateurs (and some professionals too). They tend to use their flash on the camera hot shoe or on a short bracket. The result is that the source is too near the lens axis and light reflects directly to the camera from the back of the subject's eyes. This gives the familiar 'horror-filled' red eyeballs. The best technique to avoid this is to hold the gun high and point it towards your subjects.

Fill-in (or synchro-sunlight as it sometimes is known) flash is used to lighten any harsh shadows that fall on your subjects out-of-doors. What needs to be done is a careful balancing of the daylight with the flash. This is achieved by selecting your desired lens aperture/shutter speed by taking a normal light reading, then by adding flash accordingly. This is not as simple as it sounds, because a powerful flash could well overlight the subject resulting in an overexposed photograph. Using a 'computer' type of gun the calculations are easier. If for example you select a lens aperture of *f*11 for your subject, flash balance is best if you set your gun one or two stops *less* than the camera aperture. Thus, the gun is set at either *f*5.6 or *f*8. Some automatic flashguns take into account the available light and therefore give false readings – they tend to give insufficient 'fill-in' light. The only way to overcome this problem, is by setting the gun on manual, or by using a 'variable-power' adaptor. With a manual gun you may need to work in reverse once you have taken your light reading. Your meter may inform you that your exposure should be 1/125 second at *f*11. Work out your flash exposure as you would in normal flashlit situations, i.e. divide the distance into the guide number. If you come up with the same number, *f*11, the your flash will be as bright as the sunlight. You will therefore need to modify the setting on your camera to reduce the fill-in light. Instead of setting your camera on 1/125 at *f*11 you need to adjust your setting so that the flash set at *f*11 acts just as a fill-in light. Decreasing the shutter speed and stopping down the lens aperture gives the desired setting. Now, instead of the previous camera setting, you end up with 1/60 at *f*16 on the camera, or should you want the flash fill-in to have less effect, try 1/30 at *f*22. If your camera has a focal-plane shutter then the range of shutter speeds you can use with electronic flash is restricted (usually to 1/60 second and longer). Also ensure that your camera is set on the X setting for electronic flash (on some cameras this occurs automatically).

Winter is another problem facing the social photographer. People have a disregard for the photographer's problems and decide to book their weddings for 5.00 pm on a winter's day when it is pitch dark putside. You have two alternatives; take the photographs indoors or use flash outside. It may also be too cold to do much photography outside. Flash, either computerized or manual, with your camera aperture calculated in the normal way is the only technique to adopt in this situation. You need to use a background fairly close to your subjects for the best results. Unfortunately the photographs are bound to look ghastly because your flash is the only light source, which makes them flat and harsh. If you take your subjects away from the background, the result is a picture containing a pitch black sky and darkness all around the subjects. Although this effect can be used for a few photographs, it is not so exciting if the whole series is taken in this way.

Meters and metering

Light is often tricky and requires careful and precise measurement. Some cameras are equipped with spot meters or other forms of through-the-lens metering or on-the-camera meter. These are adequate in average conditions but when a precise reading is required of a contrasty subject, a hand-held meter gives greater flexibility. The hand meter similarly is important if you intend taking a range of indoor pictures using only available light.

Most light meters today are photoelectric employing three forms of operation. The first use selenium cells which convert light energy into electrical energy which powers the meter needle across the dial. The more light there is then the more electrical current is produced and the higher the reading will be. The second type makes use of a small battery and in this case the energy is passed through a cadmium sulphide cell which acts as a resistor. This accordingly conducts current to the meter needle in much the same way as the former type. The third type uses a combination of the two methods, with silicon or selenium based cells which generate current, and a battery-powered amplifier to increase it to a level capable of display.

There are two ways of reading light. Most modern meters are equipped to read both forms. The first is *incident light,* the light that falls on the subject. Although there are those who argue differently, this form of light measurement is not greatly suited to wedding and social photography where your prime consideration is lighting people's faces. If the face is lit at a level unlike the rest of the scene, then the incident light reading can be misleading. The other form of measurement is to take a *reflected* reading. Here the photographer takes his reading from a subject. For instance, on an available light photograph taken by a window, it is best to take a light reading directly from the subject's face.

The incident light method normally employs a white translucent cone that attaches to the back of the meter. It takes into account the light falling on the subject from any direction that is likely to rebound to the camera. This is fine for most subjects – especially outdoors where the lighting is reasonably even. It is not, however, always as satisfactory in highly contrasty situations – such as when shooting by window light. In that case, the meter may be overinfluenced by the bright light streaming in through the window; or indeed, by the lack of the light reflected back from the room. In such a case, it is much better to measure from a selected area of your subject's face. In this way you can be quite sure that you are metering the light that is important to you. Without the diffusing

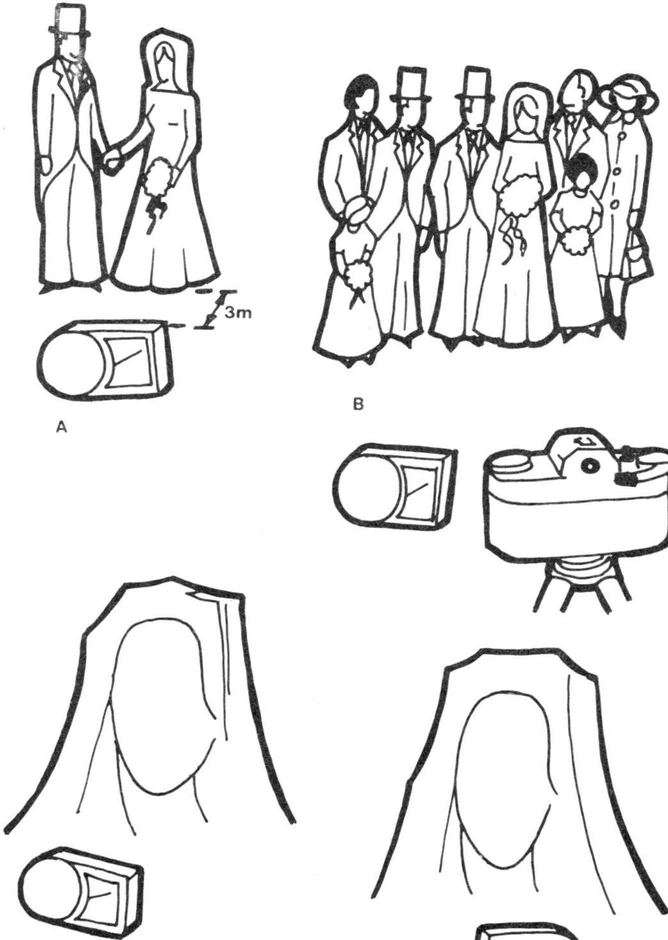

Taking an exposure meter reading. A. The contrast between the bride's dress and the groom's suit is likely to be high. An average reading is obtained if the meter is at least 3 m (10 ft) from the couple. B. Evenly lit groups which are not backlit can be metered at the camera position. C. When backlighting is present a reading close to the subject (whether one person or a group) gives a correct exposure. D. Incident light readings are excellent when the lighting is even and not too contrasty, as it is for most outside shots.

cone, the meter reads from a more clearly defined area, especially when you hold it really close to your subject.
If following the exposure reading from the brightly lit areas means that the shadows will be overdark then you must add light in them, either with fill-in flash or with a suitable reflector.

Film

Medium speed films offer the best results for social photography because they allow you to obtain excellent quality in average lighting conditions. Enlargements can be produced to substantial size without the effects of grain becoming too marked. As with cameras, make of film is left very much to the individual. Colour film is now used on the majority of weddings and most laboratories are geared up for the processing and handling of 'professional' negative films. Kodak Vericolor II is the most widely used professional colour negative film; and most laboratories can handle it. Some, though, have services available for other makes. In fact, you would be well advised to discuss film choice with your laboratory. Whatever make you choose, 100 ASA film must be the first choice; but do not overlook the newer 400 ASA materials. They can be a boon in dull conditions.
Much progress has been made in the manufacture of colour film. The faster films were introduced in recent years to cater for a wider range of conditions. Grain is less apparent and quality colour prints can be produced from a 400 ASA negative. The fast colour films are finding widespread acceptance with those engaged in wedding photography, especially during the darker months of winter.
Transparencies are something seldom considered by couples when they hire their official wedding photographer. This is somewhat strange considering the large number of amateur photographers who take slides for their own use. If you are operating unofficially at a wedding it could perhaps be a pleasant gesture to offer the couple a set of slides of the occasion.
The reversal films for transparencies available on the market range in speeds from 25 ASA to 400 ASA to cover all applications. The faster films can also be 'push processed' to give up to three stops in-

crease on their original speed rating. Thus, 400 ASA films can be rated at up to 3200 ASA for use in really poor light. Granted such 'pushing' results in a loss of quality, nevertheless some spectacular results can easily be achieved.
Many professional colour laboratories handling reversal films offer a service involving increased processing times for films that have been taken in this way.
It is best to try a few films (black-and-white and colour) to grow familiar with their characteristics before embarking on an assignment with a strange film in your camera. Once you have chosen your materials, do not change them without good reason.

The misty filter

The easiest way of producing mood inspiring 'misties' is to paint petroleum jelly around the edges of an ordinary plain glass or ultraviolet filter. Leaving the centre (just a few millimetres) of the attachment clear, place the gadget before the taking lens of your camera. Depending on the aperture chosen on your lens, you will achieve varying degrees of mist on your compositions.
This tends to be a messy way of producing an attachment. Some of the major filter makers have a selection of misty filters on the market. However, these manufactured attachments are less misty than the home-made variety. You can adapt a manufactured misty by adding layers of clear nail varnish or polystyrene glue to the surface. By building up these layers a greater depth of mist can be achieved. When used with a standard lens, an aperture of around *f* 8 usually produces a reasonable area of mist which vignettes the subject image.
If it is not overdone, mistiness adds a great deal of romance to specific wedding photographs. It is the simplest of effects to employ and is a technique that many wedding couples admire and appreciate. The addition of the misty attachment has a wide range of applications. Most commonly it is best suited to bridal or couple close-ups and to certain photographs taken during the religious wedding ceremony. For example, you can take the couple to a pleasant spot in the churchyard; where there is some greenery is best! Place the groom's left arm around his bride's waist. The bride should

hold her floral bouquet in her right hand and her left hand can be placed on top of the flowers in a way that shows her ring. The bride and groom's heads are then positioned so that they are touching and they glance down so that they are looking at the ring and the bouquet. You now have a pleasing and harmonious study which is ready for the addition of the misty filter to give a soft vignette to the composition.

Again the applications are endless for employing the misty attachment but be careful not to over use it. A little bit of effect can go a very long way – but if overdone it will cease to be something different. There is an example of the use of the misty attachment on the cover of this book.

Other lens attachments

There are many other filters and lens attachments on sale. There are colour burst attachments giving a ray of rainbow colours on photographs, multi-image prisms that produce a multi-image photograph, spot filters that give a type of misty effect with a sharp central zone, and numerous others. Some of them can work well on weddings but many tend to look out of place. Try any that interest you thoroughly before putting them into practical use on an assignment.

A close look at some advertising photography or some of the more adventurous television shows will give some idea of what kind of attachments are available and the effects they produce.

For example, you could try using a simple tube of clear plastic; the type of substance that is used for making up slides for overhead projection units. This placed in front of the lens produces a halo around the subject and gives a rather interesting effect.

When using twin-lens reflex cameras it can be rather difficult to use along with many other special effects attachments because it is not possible to judge the *exact* effect at the chosen aperture.

The starburst filter

The starburst attachment is one that is especially suited to wedding coverage. This is manufactured in various sizes and has patterns of

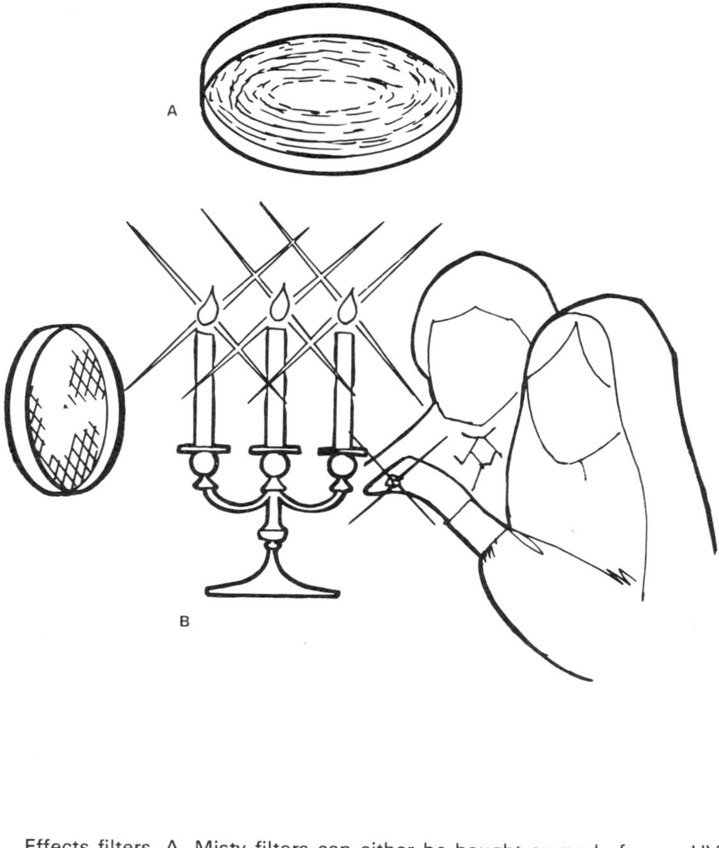

Effects filters. A. Misty filters can either be bought or made from a UV filter which has clear glue or nail varnish painted around the edge – the centre spot remaining clear. The amount of mistiness depends on the substance coated and its thickness, the radius of the filter left clear, and the lens aperture used. Wide apertures give the greatest effect. (Front cover of this book was photographed using a misty filter). B. Starburst filters have a fine grid pattern engraved on them. The number of points coming from the lights in the scene, such as candles, varies according to the filter used and is commonly 4, 6, or 8.

lines criss-crossed on the glass surface. Varying patterns of lines engraved on the filter give a differing number of 'bursts' when aimed at a point of light.

Commonly these attachments are available in four, six or eight points. The patterns of lines act as a dispersant of light, radiating it into bursts like a star. As an example, a starburst filter can be attached to the camera lens when a candle is in the scene. The image of the candle flame is split into a burst of light with long extending rays 'bursting' into four, six or eight separate rays of light (depending on which particular starburst you are using). The effect can make a startling change from a straightforward photograph. However, you must take care not to overuse such an attachment.

When you photograph the interior of a church, a starburst can be used to pick up the light points of candles that are placed on the altar. A straight shot without the aid of a starburst does not always look very interesting. By adding the special attachment, greater interest is given to an otherwise standard composition.

Candles always add a touch of romance when used in bridal subjects. The bride, when lit by candlelight in a subtle way, makes a fine portrait. Again, the starburst can be added for greater effect. The star effects are more marked when working closer to the sources of light and therefore a portrait of this sort contains very noticeable rays of light bursting from the candle flames. Take care, by turning the attachment on the lens, to place the rays of bursting light so that they are not cutting across the bride's face.

Matte boxes and multi-exposures

Today, in order to remain at the top as a wedding photographer, you need to devote some of your time studying the various effects that can be created within the camera by using double and multi-exposures. The public are not only growing more aware about what is good and what is bad photography, but more especially they are looking towards a record of their weddings that is 'different'. Customers have found a taste for special effects and an increasing number of couples are asking their photographers to produce something away from the average coverage.

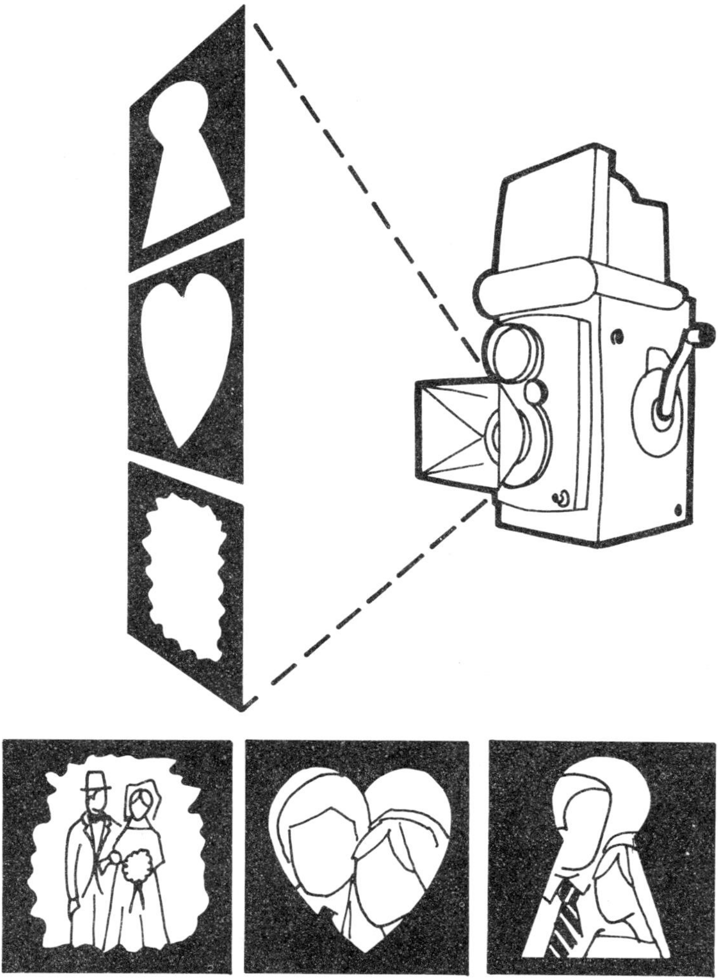

The matte box. A deep lens hood can be adapted to take a series of masks or you can buy ready-made masks and holders. Experimentation is needed to determine the best position of the mask and the most suitable lens aperture.

From the USA extends the creative flair of photographers such as Rocky Gunn and Jack Curtis. These wedding craftsmen make extensive use of what is known as the 'matte box' to create multi-images and their work has become so well known that they have given successful seminars on the subject on both sides of the Atlantic.

Basically a matte box is a derivation of a professional style camera lens hood adapted so that it can hold a variety of masks and inserts. When placed before the camera lens, these inserts give a range of interesting visual effects. For example; it is possible to use masks which prevent an area of the negative from being exposed. A second exposure, using a mask which 'protects' the area of negative exposed in the previous shot, is then taken so that a second image is made on the negative in the exact situation that you want it.

The uses of the matte box are wide and varied. It can be used to 'superimpose' the couple within a brandy glass or it can similarly be used to 'float' the couple above the altar. Experiment thoroughly with the possibilities that can be achieved.

Pre-cut masks can also be placed before the lens to produce various shapes that can be used to frame the bride and groom. It is thus possible to shoot the couple within a key hole, heart, oval or any other shape that can be cut from a small mask.

There are a growing number of matte boxes available on the market. These are chiefly advertised in the professional photographic journals and most of the manufacturers produce illustrated brochures showing the effects that can be accomplished. A small booklet also normally comes with a purchased matte box and this explains in detail how the various effects can be produced.

If you are fairly useful at do-it-yourself, you could probably make your own matte box, and also save money, by adapting a lens hood and cutting your own masks.

Another way of achieving similar double exposures is to use a standard background negative which can be used for double printing by a commercial laboratory. In the USA these are more readily available than in the UK and include such backgrounds as a prayer book and sheet music. The subjects are then printed over the top in an area that has been left blank on the negative in much the same way as the masks prevent an area of negative from being exposed when using the matte box.

Some colour laboratories also produce superimposed montage prints that use the combination of two or more negatives to give a double image effect.

Exactly how far you dare go with special effects is a matter of choice. Several laboratories now offer a double printing method of obtaining multi-images. The laboratory-produced effects at least offer any photographer the chance of providing his customers with special-effect photographs but in many ways, because the labs make use of stock negatives, the system is contrived and less authentic.

Multi-images have largely been overplayed now that almost every wedding photographer includes them within his range. The situation has now arisen that several photographers in any one area may be offering exactly the same studies. This emphasizes the need for each photographer to develop his own style which can be produced at camera stage with a minimum of effort and without the need for using mass-produced print aids.

Preparation for Wedding Photography

Most weddings take many months to plan before everything is ready for the 'big day'. Considering the many people that are brought together to provide various services on the wedding day, it is surprising that so few weddings are ruined as a result of something being missing from the occasion.
It takes very little to ruin a wedding. Imagine the bride's disappointment if her limousine fails to turn up! Similarly, if the photographer happens to blunder and his photographs fail to come out the result is the same – a happy occasion destroyed through negligence.
The photographer has the most difficult task to perform on the day. Not only is his work made harder by the possibility of inclement weather but there also remains the strong probability of something going wrong with his equipment. Most equipment breakdowns can be attributed to errors on the photographer's part – a few however are unavoidable when a key part of a camera fails. The latter are going to happen no matter whatever prior preparations you make. The former, however, can easily be avoided by commonsense and a check on all items of equipment before the wedding.

Routine equipment checks

The photographer owes it to his clients to ensure that everything possible has been done to reduce the risk of the results not coming out. The first thing to be done is to ensure that your electronic flash is functioning in synchronization with the camera. To do this take your camera indoors without a film in it. With a diaphragm (between-the-lens) shutter camera, set the lens at fullest (widest) aperture and open the back, pointing the lens towards a light-coloured wall. Direct your electronic flash gun at the same wall and plug the lead into the 'X' sync socket on the camera. Look into the back of the camera and fire the gun by depressing the camera shutter button. If you see a complete white circle of light through the lens then your camera is in sync with the flash gun. If however, you do *not* see a clear circle but can also see the silhouette of part of the camera shutter blades, then your camera is faulty and must be looked at by an expert.

If your camera has a focal-plane shutter (as have virtually all recent 35 mm SLRs) the procedure is similar. You must, though, select the correct shutter speed (usually 1/60 or 1/125 second). Some models have the flash synchronization adjusted by the shutter-speed dial; others have only X-synchronization. Take the lens off altogether. When you test the flash, you must be able to see the entire picture area (film gate) illuminated. If not, either you have selected too fast a shutter speed, or your camera needs adjusting. At the same time you can ensure that your camera synchronization leads are not broken. By keeping the lead plugged into the 'X' socket on the camera and checking to see that the camera shutter is being operated on the correct speed for flash synchronization, fire the flash several times by pressing the camera shutter button. Allow sufficient time for the flash to recycle before each firing and if at any time the flash gun refuses to fire at once then there is the probability that a wire has broken or cracked in the sync lead.

Regular 'check-ups' should be given to all your photographic equipment. This involves the stripping down of the equipment by trained mechanics and the replacement of any faulty or potentially damaged parts. The shutter is also put through a series of electronically timed tests to ensure that it is operating at the various speeds or as near to them as makes little difference. Unfortunately, many photographers are reluctant to have their cameras serviced at regular intervals because of the cost. It is easy to become rather complacent until such time as equipment gives up completely and you have to have it repaired or opt for a new piece. Frequently the delay in having cameras serviced is a false economy.

Trouble shooting

One of the commonest causes of photographic failure at social events is created by photographers who shoot their rolls of film using flash but with their cameras out of synchronization. The way to check your camera has already been described but several well-known cameras frequently used at weddings can be knocked out of sync by accident.

Such cameras are fitted with a synchronization switch or lever that moves between 'X' sync (correct for electronic flash) and 'M' sync (for flash-bulbs). The 'M' setting is a short delay (about 20 milliseconds) between the shutter being released and the flash-bulb being fired. (Flash-bulbs are virtually redundant for most photographic purposes.) If you are using electronic flash and the sync switch is accidentally set to 'M', the net result is no exposure where electronic flash is the only light source and no fill-in for out-side shots.

The lesson is clear. Each photographer should check and recheck his switch frequently during the taking of a series of photographs. On some cameras, you can tape the switch in position with no loss of convenience.

Flash leads also have the habit of playing up especially during humid weather when they seem more likely to break inside. Always carry a spare in case of this happening.

Cameras are of course expensive and in your early days of wedding operating you may not be able to afford a second camera for emergencies. If you work with 6 × 6 cm ($2\frac{1}{4} \times 2\frac{1}{4}$ in) equipment and have a 35 mm camera as well, take it along and have it ready loaded with colour negative stock as a back-up. Even though your particular laboratory may not handle small negatives for wedding work, in the event of your main 120 roll-film camera breaking down then the 35 mm serves as a standby and you can always get the results processed elsewhere.

While on the subject of 35 mm cameras the common fault concerning the film winding must be mentioned. There are stories of wedding operators working with 35 mm equipment who have come unstuck on a job because the film in their cameras had split on the ratchet holes. The first they knew of their mistake was when the film failed to stop winding once they had exhausted the 36 exposures on the cassette. Horror of horrors! When they opened the backs of their cameras they found that the film was not advancing, their efforts had been wasted and the client was extremely annoyed.

It is easy to avoid this happening. When you wind the film on using the film advance lever, the camera rewind knob also turns as the film advances. If the knob fails to turn then you should test first that the film is taut. If it is and the knob still is not turning as the film transport is advanced then the film is torn on the ratchet holes.

Another possible trouble source are films that have no adhesive on the tail ends with which to seal them up for processing. When you are using roll-film and this happens what are you to do? You cannot finish your job with a roll of exposed film held tightly between your fingers. The answer is to take along a supply of rubber bands or adhesive tape.

If you use rechargeable electronic flash guns, you must ensure that the gun has been fully charged before use. If it uses wet cells, then keep them topped. Similarly with battery-operated units, check to see if the batteries have sufficient power reserves to see you through a wedding. If not then they must be replaced. A wise precaution is to use a new set of batteries for each job, or at least take some with you.

Always carry a small pocket flashgun as well to get you out of trouble, if your normal flash fails.

Assessing the location

If you are confident that your equipment is functioning correctly the next stage of preparation involves an early look at the location of the wedding. If the church or civic centre is local you will lose nothing by taking time to go and have a look at the place.

You must learn to seek out any suitable backgrounds that can be utilized to enhance your photographs. This can sometimes be difficult especially for photographers working in built-up areas where a large number of churches have been built facing directly onto a main highway. Even in new towns and cities, the churches have been designed to include very little in the way of landscaping. The photographer has very little choice and has to work with whatever is available.

Brick walls are stark and look grim when they are used as backdrops for photographs. There are, however, even worse backgrounds

– coloured doors and windows, for example, may clash with people's clothes. Nothing looks worse than a group of brides-maids in cornflower-coloured dresses against a vivid blue-green church door.

You should be looking for areas of natural foliage, pleasantly styled arches, statues, fountains and garden seats. The list of possible backgrounds is endless; it is up to the photographer to use the best suited for his photographs.

When trees and small bushes are available use them. If you look at a cross-section of wedding photography, you will commonly find a large number of photographs taken against the church door or side wall. This can be the case even when more suitable backgrounds are readily found just yards away. If better areas exist for photography use them, your compositions will benefit enormously.

Spend a little time walking around the grounds of the wedding location. A notebook can be handy for the novice photographer. Note down the possibilities and before the wedding party arrives decide in your own mind where each of your photographs will be taken.

Lychgates are found at many older churches. These can be used to frame the couple especially when they are posed looking back over their shoulders at you as they prepare to leave for their reception.

If nothing really can be found other than a wall, then try to reduce the impact the brick or concrete may have by turning your subjects at an angle from it rather than shooting them flat against the surface. Try and bring your subjects as far forward as possible to fill the frame of your camera.

Planning the coverage

There is little point in arriving at a wedding without any idea of how you are going to cover the occasion. Naturally early inexperience will show to some degree but this can be reduced by learning your 'shooting script' thoroughly. You can then determine where you will shoot each photograph when you look around the location before the wedding. Never leave anything to chance; try to work out in your own mind how you want to handle the occasion. If you have clear ideas then your task will become much easier and your operations smoother in all respects.

The shooting script mentioned above is described more fully in later sections. Basically it is devised around the traditional standard photographs that *must* be taken and for ease is listed by the photographer in order of taking, building from small pictures, such as the couple full-length, towards the largest family groups.
If you know what you are doing the whole process of covering a wedding will go by without a hitch and your subjects will have greater confidence in your ability. Do not leave it to the couple to tell you what photographs to take. They can offer suggestions but never allow them to direct your operations. *You* must be seen to be the expert and therefore it is *you* that must call the order of photographs as you want them.
Do not be afraid to write out a list of subjects in the correct order of taking. Keep your list simple and easy to read so that it can be used for quick reference at any time during your work. Tape the list to your camera or tripod so that you always have it handy to remind you of any photographs that you may not have included.

Dressing for the occasion

If you attend a wedding as a guest it is quite natural for you to dress according to the occasion. The same rule applies when you attend someone else's wedding as the official photographer. It is only good manners and commonsense to dress smartly yet it is astounding how many photographers do not make the effort. Your manner and appearance will be taken as a reflection of the work you produce.

Working with People

Guests are not always predictable and camera shyness is a human characteristic you may often encounter. If a guest does not wish to participate in a group photograph then there is no point in forcing the issue. Be polite, back down and respect the guest's wishes not to be photographed.

The church

Priests, clergymen, and church vergers (hereafter referred to in the text as priests) can be antagonistic towards photographers, but more often than not they are kind, courteous and helpful. You will learn that it pays to be respectful when dealing with them. In the UK many are strong on the point of refusing the photographer permission to cover any part of the religious ceremony. The attitude elsewhere may vary from enthusiastic encouragement, even holding up or repeating parts of the service for your benefit, to strong condemnation. Many photographers feel that the couple should have the right to choose whether or not their ceremony is covered photographically. After all, it is a tender ceremony that should be preserved on film providing the photographer acts in keeping with the occasion and works without intrusion. It is wise to introduce yourself to the priest when you arrive at the church before beginning coverage. You lose nothing by asking his permission to take photographs during the ceremony. Always emphasize that flash will *not* be used apart from during the signing of the marriage register and when the couple walk back up the church aisle.
The problems have to be examined from both sides. Photographers are not perfect. Many wedding operators refuse to ask permission to use their cameras in church and in so doing damage the attitude of a reasonable priest.

If you succeed in obtaining permission to cover any part of the ceremony, you must ensure that you do not overstep the mark. Photograph *only* those parts of the ceremony for which you have been granted permission. Respect the priest's wishes and you will be doing a favour to more people than yourself.

The bride and bridegroom

It is natural for couples to be nervous on their wedding day so take this into consideration if they appear anxious. To take the best pictures you need to induce some calm into the atmosphere. Reassure the couple that what you are doing is really in their interests. Be sincere in your approach and ensure them that you are *really* working for them and not for your own ego.

While you are taking your photographs of the couple try to tell them exactly what you are doing. This does not mean that you should go into a lengthy discussion about the purpose of your chosen '*f*' stop; but try and keep up a lively banter of interesting conversation that will hold their attention. This can be more difficult than it sounds, especially if you are a novice wedding operator, because you can find it awkward to concentrate on what you are doing while making conversation. In time, as your camera controls and posing of your subjects becomes second nature, you will find this easy.

As the official photographer you must take control of the situation as soon as the couple and their guests leave the church. If you let things take their course then it is difficult for you to recover from the surrounding celebrations in order to take your photographs. Furthermore you quickly lose the respect of the couple and their guests. You are employed to take photographs and therefore you must ensure that your task is performed as quietly and efficiently as possible.

On most occasions you will have met the couple before the wedding so they will be familiar to you. Try to establish some common form of interest you may share with them, so that talk can revolve around that interest to keep them occupied while you set up your shots. Any small talk helps to establish an understanding. A sense of humour is vital, but do not allow your comments to become rude

(although on some occasions you will find the remarks made at you can be!)

It is vital to give the impression of caring about the occasion. One of the biggest mistakes made by wedding photographers is that they forget the true meaning of the occasion and this shows in the photographs taken. Weddings are romantic and moving occasions. Try to capture this tenderness through the photographs you take. The wedding photographer that learns this art is destined for success!

Talk quietly, gently and precisely to the couple and encourage them in every way to pose as you direct them.

There is no harm in asking them if there are any special photographs that they would like taken. You will be appreciated for taking the trouble to ask but take care that their requests do not dominate the proceedings. It is best to point out that you start by taking the standard formal photographs and then take them aside for a selection of informal studies. It is at this time that you can ask if they have any special people they would like to be photographed with.

Most brides will be delighted with the way you have portrayed them, but from the start you must overcome any anxieties they may show. Offer encouragement, make pleasant – but sincere – remarks about the way they look and chat to them to keep their minds off the camera. The majority of brides react favourably towards a warm and friendly photographer who takes a genuine interest.

Occasionally there is a couple who seem to worry more than most. They may attempt to tell you in what order you should take your pictures. Smile, be friendly, listen to what they have to say then explained that you are working to a well-tested system. Inform them that you will take any specially requested photographs at the end of your set routine. Usually this satisfies the couple and convinces them that you *do* know what you are doing and that you are unlikely to forget to take any key photographs.

The bride and groom are normally happy to pose as you suggest and you should not experience many problems. The secret is to keep smiling, be friendly and to work with the utmost enthusiasm and efficiency. If you remember these points then your photographs will turn out as you want them to. Do remember, though, that you are attending *their* ceremony; you are not arranging a group of models to suit your own photographic ends.

Handling parents

Like the bride and groom, the parents are frequently nervous. They may have had to carry the burden of planning the wedding and it is natural that they should be concerned about anything going wrong. If you have not already met the parents, try to make a point of introducing yourself as soon as they arrive at the ceremony. The groom's parents normally arrive first, followed by the bride's mother (except in Jewish weddings). The father of the bride normally accompanies his daughter in the bridal limousine.

Express friendship towards the parents and be relatively informal. This usually brings a warm response and helps relieve some of their tensions. Reassure them that you are well versed in wedding coverage and express your desire to meet any special requests that they may have. If you request the father's help when setting up group photographs this too may help establish yourself as a friend and break down any customer–photographer barrier that may exist.

The bride's mother can be overprotective. She may insist on arranging the bride's gown or in rearranging your efforts after you have so painstakingly set it to suit your composition. You must be understanding. Gently inform her that you have set the dress with a particular intention in mind but she is welcome to help you arrange it.

Your handling of the parents is based very much on your tact and ability to instill confidence. Once they are satisfied that you can cope and that you operate in a professional manner then your dealings should run smoothly. A certain amount of small talk and the paying of the odd compliment, if sincere, will generally ensure that they work with you rather than against you. Remember that the parents will be amongst your biggest critics. If you please them then they can become your closest allies when it comes to collecting your orders.

Problems with groups

Groups may be a problem. Many photographers, especially when they are training to become wedding operators, are frightened by groups. Certainly very large weddings can involve worries for the photographer because of the magnitude of people. But group arranging need not be difficult.

By keeping calm and by enlisting the help of the parents, groups small and large, can be constructed with ease,

It may be necessary to adopt a firm attitude. Clap your hands, call out your requests and lead guests into position in a friendly encouraging way. You may find that there are guests that never respond. These are best left out of your photograph or, as an alternative, can be coaxed into place by the bride and groom at your request. The frustrations of group building can be overcome providing you remain good-tempered.

Keep your dealings at a personal level and do not be afraid to pay compliments to guests as you show them their position within a group. A patient photographer receives much greater accolade than one who goes about his work like a bull running through a china shop.

Occasionally all your efforts to set up a group may fail. If this does happen, and you have tried your best, then accept defeat gracefully. The couple usually understands your problems and may not be too concerned. If they still insist on having groups taken, in the rare event of lack of cooperation on the part of the guests, you need to take a firm line and ensure that the bride's father and best man do the arranging with you.

As you gain experience then so your ability to handle groups increases and you will find that in time the various idiosyncrasies of wedding guests will be easier to tolerate.

Working with the registrar

Civil wedding ceremonies in the UK are an alternative to religious ceremonies. Elsewhere, the civil ceremony is mandatory regardless of whether or not there is a church wedding.

Generally the ceremony is short, about ten to fifteen minutes and the photographer is not allowed to take his photographs during the course of the actual ceremony. Although, a quick word at the start with the registrar or his or her assistant ensures cooperation for the photographic session immediately following the formalities.

Different registrars have their own way of handling matters. It is usual for the whole ceremony to be conducted; and then the photographer allowed to pose the couple signing the marriage register, placing their rings and giving one another a celebratory kiss once the formalities have been completed.

In some cases the registrar stops the ceremony at the appropriate moment to allow you the opportunity of capturing the couple as the rings are placed. In this case the signing of the register will still be posed after the completion of the formalities.

Nowadays civil weddings, frequently held in special marriage rooms at town halls, are far more personal than they once were. This type of wedding is very popular and in many ways couples prefer the quick ceremony to the longer ritual that is associated with church weddings.

Most registrars and their staff are experienced at their jobs and appreciate the importance of photography at a wedding and therefore are helpful providing you observe the rules and do not attempt to take photographs at the wrong moments.

Chauffeurs, caterers and toastmasters

The photographer does cross the path of other people who provide services at weddings. Therefore it is important to establish a happy working relationship with others because if you work regularly in the same area you are likely to meet them again.

One problem for the wedding photographer can be the chauffeur who is overbooked. In the peak wedding season some car hire firms are notorious for booking their cars to tight schedules. On occasions you find a chauffeur in a panic because he is late to collect a bride for his next wedding. You may sometimes be asked to speed up your work to help him out. Of course, if you are able to save a few minutes during your coverage to assist then so much the better. If you are 'told' by chauffeurs that you simply cannot take any photographs at the church because they have to get to another wedding, then you must press on regardless and complete your work. Obviously it is best to avoid confrontations when this happens; but the couple and their guests have every right to expect you to take as much care as usual and not to hurry your work.

On the other hand, the chauffeur is just as likely to help you set up the shots involving his car and if the weather is bad you may find him holding an umbrella for you.

Chauffeurs hate to have confetti thrown at their cars – and with good reason. It is extremely difficult to clean from car interiors and, especially during wet weather, sticks to the bodywork of the car. It is best to take a confetti photograph as far away as possible from the car, and of course, away from the church lawns which is another source of irritation with priests.

Your dealings with caterers are less likely to create problems. A word with the head caterer when you arrive at the reception helps to delay the guests being received while you complete the cake-cutting and toasting photographs. Similarly if the weather forces you to complete your photographs at the reception it is wise to ask the caterers not to serve drinks until your work is done. Once guests can take a drink your task becomes increasingly difficult because their interest in photography suddenly wanes.

Caterers can also assist you to move obstructive tables and chairs, and often set up the cake-cutting photograph ready for you to take. They can also be very helpful when you return to the reception and not only provide a table or space for you to 'sell your services' but frequently keep you replenished in drinks and food. Good caterers can be worth their weight in gold and a good understanding not only brings you valuable help at the reception but may also lead to a caterer recommending you for further commissions.

Toastmasters can also be most helpful. They are usually born organizers and can offer you a lot of assistance. They can arrange 'natural breaks' to enable you to take your key photographs and may help in setting up groups of people needed for a particular photograph.

Lastly, the band or discotheque which provides the reception with music can also be useful when you return to the reception with the proofs. They can announce your arrival on the public address system and keep the guests posted of your whereabouts which saves you time.

Good relationships between the various wedding contractors can only lead to benefits for all and therefore it is wise for you to build-up an understanding with other organizations.

The Western Church Wedding – Before the Ceremony

Church weddings in the West commonly follow traditional patterns. Of course there are variations from country to country, from denomination to denomination, and from town to town. This chapter first looks at a standard fairly organized ceremony, which is quite similar in all denominations, and then goes on to discuss the differences in civil ceremonies, and in one or two other religions. Whatever persuasion the couple follow, their wedding pictures take the same sort of pattern. Whenever you come across a special practice, ask the couple just what special photographs they need.

Wedding coverage can be broken down into various defined stages. By choice or because of the confines within their working organization, not every professional photographer includes every facet within his repertoire. However, you will probably learn most by becoming involved in all stages of a wedding.

Basically these stages of coverage are as follows:

1 The bride at home.
2 The guests' and parents' arrivals.
3 The bride's arrival.
4 The ceremony.
5 After the ceremony.
6 Couple's departure.
7 The reception.
8 Final departures.

Within these stages fall the two main ways of dealing with the picture making – formal coverage and casual coverage. If you do decide on the more casual style do make sure that you at least give some formal coverage as this is usually appreciated by the more traditional person.

The bride at home

Most wedding photographers try to give their customers the 'full works'. They therefore usually begin by visiting the bride at her home a short while before she leaves for the ceremony. This allows you to include a selection of very worthwhile portraits of the bride, her close family and her attendants in a somewhat more leisurely atmosphere than is possible at the church or at the reception.
By taking these shots you may also help the bride to relax before what is, after all, something of an ordeal. It also accustoms the bride and her family to the camera; which of course leads to better understanding when it comes to taking the main photographs after the ceremony.
In order to simplify this section of the book, each of the prescribed stages of coverage is listed before going on to describe the methods of posing for each. The bride at home stage should include some or all of the following compositions.

Bride at dressing table.
Bride close-up.
Bride full-length.
Bride with mother.
Bride with attendants.
Attendants alone.
Bride with both parents.
Bride with close family (i.e. parents, brothers, sisters, etc.)
Bride leaving home.

The bride in close-up

Many photographers prefer to work with available daylight whenever possible. This usually involves the use of a sturdy tripod because you are likely to be employing slow shutter speeds.
The play of light on the bride cast from one side through a window can enhance the mood of your composition. A straight flash photograph would give even illumination but the contrast provide by window light is far more endearing. There are several ways to photograph a bride close up. Each can be staged by available light.

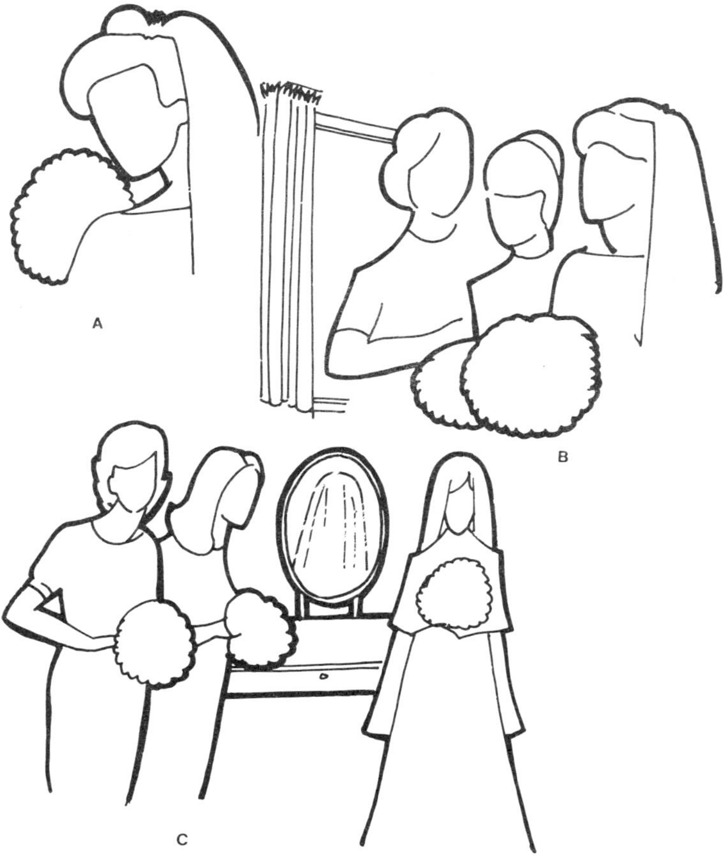

The bride at home. A. Look for new angles, perhaps with the bride looking back over her shoulder towards the camera. B. The bride and her mother or chief bridesmaid can be photographed by light from a window. C. One possible arrangement for photographing the bride with her attendants.

It is important to ensure that the bride holds her floral bouquet so that the back or handle of the bouquet is not seen and the array of flowers is clearly displayed.

Each close-up is staged near to a window where sufficient daylight illuminates her face. You can place the bouquet high, cupped in both her hands and close to her face. Turn the bride's head downwards so that she is photographed looking at or even smelling the flowers. Be careful when placing the hands; they must be arranged so that they do not intrude on the composition.

Your meter reading is taken very carefully, close to the bride's face. Of course, there is a strong contrast between the two sides, one in shadow the other, nearest the window, well-lit. Try to create a happy medium by exposing to retain the contrast and try not to overexpose by setting your camera for the lower light reading. A little underexposure retains the shadow detail and results in a more inspired photograph. Select your aperture by taking the average light reading between the shadow and well-lit sides of the bride's face. For example, if the lit side registers an aperture of *f*8 on the meter and the shadow side *f*4, the use of an aperture of *f*5.6 gives an exposure which retains the desired balance of light.

If you want to lighten the shadow side of the face you could either try adding a little flash bounced from a wall to that side of the face, or, you could use a white card reflector which bounces back some of the window light.

Expression is a key factor in any portrait. A serious thoughtful mood can enhance one of your studies. For another try asking the bride to give a radiant smile.

While there is nothing wrong in photographing the bride as a full face portrait, variation to the theme gives a more acceptable series of pictures. Try shooting your bride semi-profile or even full profile of she has sufficient strength in her facial structure. Place her bouquet in varying positions. It can be held high so that you frame your composition tightly. It can similarly be placed lower so that the bride's head is tilted further forward to look at the flowers. The possibilities are endless and need exploiting.

A really tightly framed shot of the bride can also work extremely well. Do not aim to include her whole face in the photograph, but frame your composition so that only a part of her face completely

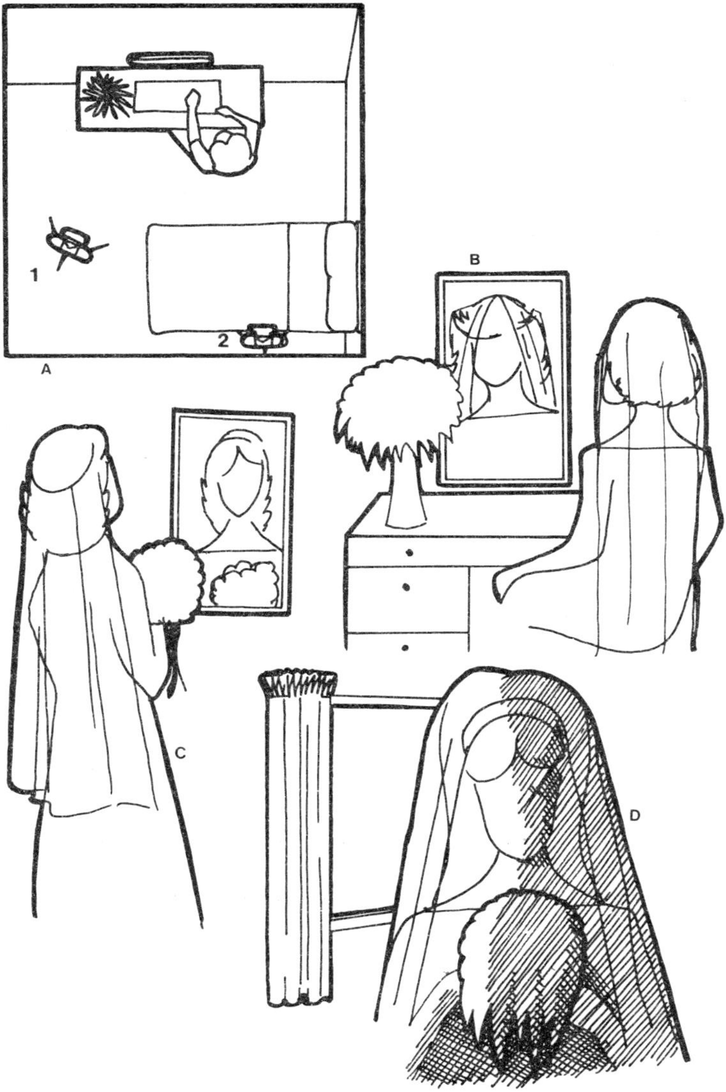

The mirror shot. A. Suitable positions for the camera are 1 and 2. B. Flash is usually required and remember to shoot at an angle to avoid reflections. You can focus on the mirror image of the bride herself depending on the desired result. C. Alternatively, effect is obtained if you pose the bride against the window and expose for the light outside.

fills the negative. Again, as with the previous studies which have been taken to include all of the bride's head, the soft daylight from a window can greatly enhance the portrait.

The bride full-length

A good full-length shot is not always possible in the home; especially if the room is small and fully furnished. This is usually the case if you work in a big crowded city. If you cannot take the photograph inside you may have to go out to the garden; or take the photograph later on at the ceremony.

Avoid the flat-on type of full-length study which unfortunately is still often taken. The whole purpose and idea behind the full-length bridal portrait is to emphasize the style of the dress. It is one of the most difficult shots to pose and the one study which many photographers get wrong.

If the gown flows well, a good way of showing the styling is to shoot from the back. Arrange the dress to its best advantage and ask the bride to walk slowly forward. If she turns from the waist towards the camera the dress will flow naturally onto the ground. As an alternative, keep the same pose but with the bride turning her head downwards in a thoughtful expression.

When the gown has no train, then it is best to shoot at a three-quarter angle with the bride placing her foot nearest the camera a little in front of the other. Her weight should be placed on her back foot. It is essential to make sure that the toes of her shoes are just visible, it will give the impression that she does indeed have feet!

A dress which does have a train can also be handled from a three-quarter view. Raise the bride's foot nearest to the camera to a tip-toe position. This bends her knee and allows the dress to follow the contours of her leg. The pose will look less rigid and the gown more stylish than if the bride was posed squarely with both feet firmly on the ground.

The hands are as important in a full-length study as they are in a close-up (when they are included). Just where you place the hands depends largely on the style of the dress. They can be placed on the bouquet and held in front of the gown; but take care that they do not

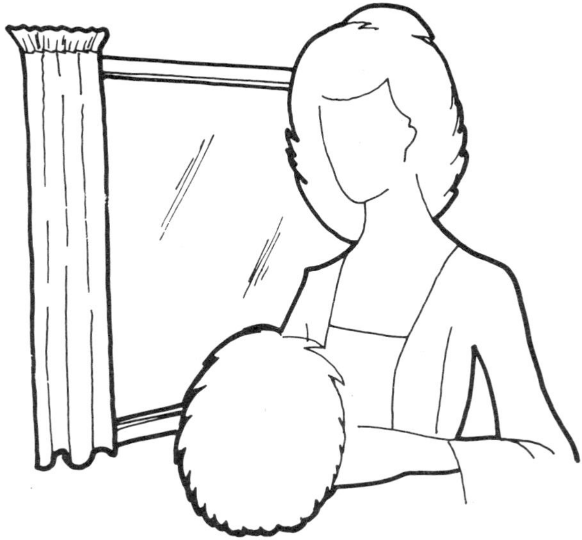

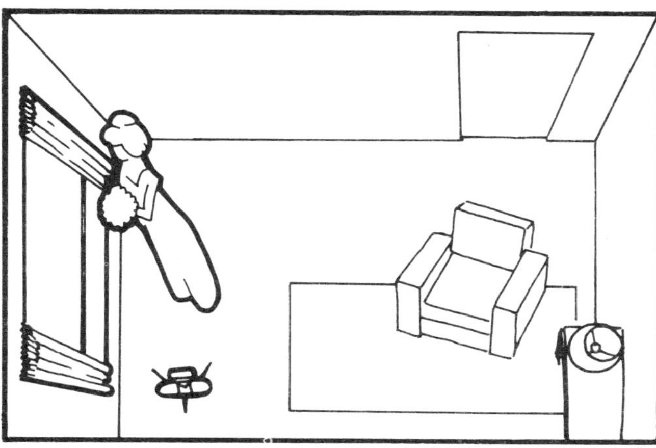

The window shot. The bride is placed near a window so that available light falls on $\frac{3}{4}$ of her face. Bounce flash fill-in can be used to soften the shadows. If a shutter speed longer than 1/60 second is employed then the camera should be mounted on a tripod.

hide any intricate lacework or patterning on the dress waist and bodice. Some photographers feel that the bride's hands must always be firmly clasped before her. This does not have to be the case, she can, for example, hold back part of the veil or train or leave them hanging by her side.
The possibilities of posing the bride full-length are almost endless. The photographer can only really determine the best method from assessing the bride and her outfit on the day. However some of the quality fashion magazines can teach the photographer a great deal and spare moments are well spent studying the pages of *Brides and Setting Up Home* (UK), *Modern Brides* (USA), *Elle, Vogue* and others.

Bride with mother

Commonly the bride and mother are photographed rigidly looking directly into the camera lens. This is acceptable but a great deal more interest can be achieved through a little bit of imaginative thinking. Hands again crop up as a problem. The bride generally has her bouquet to hang on to. Her mother may feel awkward not knowing quite where to put those itchy fingers.
One simple solution is to stage a composition which involves the mother handing the bride her floral bouquet. The bride can be either standing or seated. You should aim to bring the heads of mother and daughter onto a similar plane so that they fit comfortably into your composition without looking top-heavy.
A point often forgotten in this pose is to have the bouquet the right way round. If the mother is seen presenting the flowers to her daughter and the back and handle of the bouquet are nearest to the mother then it will not look right. Place the flowers in the mother's hands so that the back is turned towards the bride. It will then look as if she is *really* about to take the bouquet from her mother rather than vice versa. In wedding photography, the small details, such as this, can be extremely important.
The bride can also be seated with her mother standing behind her, placing her hands on the veil or head-dress as if she is making last minute adjustments. Obviously, the expressions should emphasize that they are both happy.

At the dressing table

The dressing table shot is now considered rather 'old hat' nevertheless it is still well worth including in your coverage. Few people understand how it is possible to take this photograph without getting a flash reflection or the photographer reflected in the mirror and many view this photograph as 'magic'. It is therefore vital to ensure that you do *not* appear somewhere in the picture. It is essential therefore to shoot at an angle from the glass. By using your flash at the same angle (preferably bounced) you are able to prevent an ugly 'feedback' of light associated with head on shots at glass or similar surfaces.

A round ornate mirror is sometimes found in the hallway or sitting room in many houses. If one can be found of a suitable height for the bride this can make a rather decorative shot as an alternative to the dressing table version. A profile with the bride posed very close to the mirror works well when both reflected and actual images can be seen. If there is not sufficient available daylight to allow an exposure of the desired depth of field, try bounced or even direct flash (aimed at an angle to the mirror surface).

Full-length mirror shots in wardrobe doors can also be taken. Again, the bride should be close to the glass, looking at herself in the mirror. Another way, when there is plenty of space, is to bring her away from the mirror and turn her head towards the camera. Be sure to set the dress if it is included in your framing so that you see both the front and the back of the gown in the composition.

With all mirror shots be careful about the backgrounds in the room. Bride's bedrooms are generally full of all sorts of rubbish on wedding days. Clear away any items that you see in the viewfinder which may mar the composition.

When using computer flash it may be necessary to increase your camera aperture by a $\frac{1}{2}$ stop. This compensates for any underexposure in the reflected mirror image of the bride caused by the flash sensor cutting the light output too soon. This is caused because the sensor reads the light reflected directly from the bride's real image which is nearer to the camera, than from the mirror surface.

A small aperture should also be chosen, say *f*8 or *f*11, in order that sharp focus can be given to both the real and the reflected image of the bride. It is best to focus for the mirror image.

Bride with attendants

The bride and her attendants can of course be photographed after the ceremony or as they arrive at the church or register office. Equally more relaxed pictures taken during the home session can be rewarding.

Commonly the bride is seated at her dressing table but turned to face into the bedroom rather than looking into the mirror. Place the bridesmaids and page boy (if there is one) around her and the composition is taken with your subjects smiling at the camera. This simple rendering can be a very pleasing study.

Perhaps the chief bridesmaid (or maid of honour) can be placed behind the bride, posed so that she is doing something to the head dress or tidying the bride's hair. The other attendants can be turned to watch the elder bridesmaid. This pose avoids the usual shot which depicts everyone smiling directly at the camera lens.

Town photographers often face the same old problem – lack of space. If you cannot use a garden and the rooms are too small, then there is little alternative but to shoot in close or leave the photograph until later on.

One favourite pose is to take the attendants in the same way as described for the close-up of the bride. Using the area around a softly lit window the photographer may opt for the same available daylight treatment and takes his light reading from the subjects' faces.

If the bride has a large number of attendants then this composition can be difficult. However, with two or three bridesmaids of similar height it can work admirably. Pose the bridesmaids on their own or with the bride facing towards the window in a three-quarter close-up. The attendants can also be taken in much the same way as the bride alone – posed looking at their bouquets. In each case lighting is by available daylight with, if required, a little bit of lift from a flash gun bounced from the ceiling.

A casual way of picturing the bride with her attendants is to take the shot in the lounge of her home using a sofa or similar piece of fur-

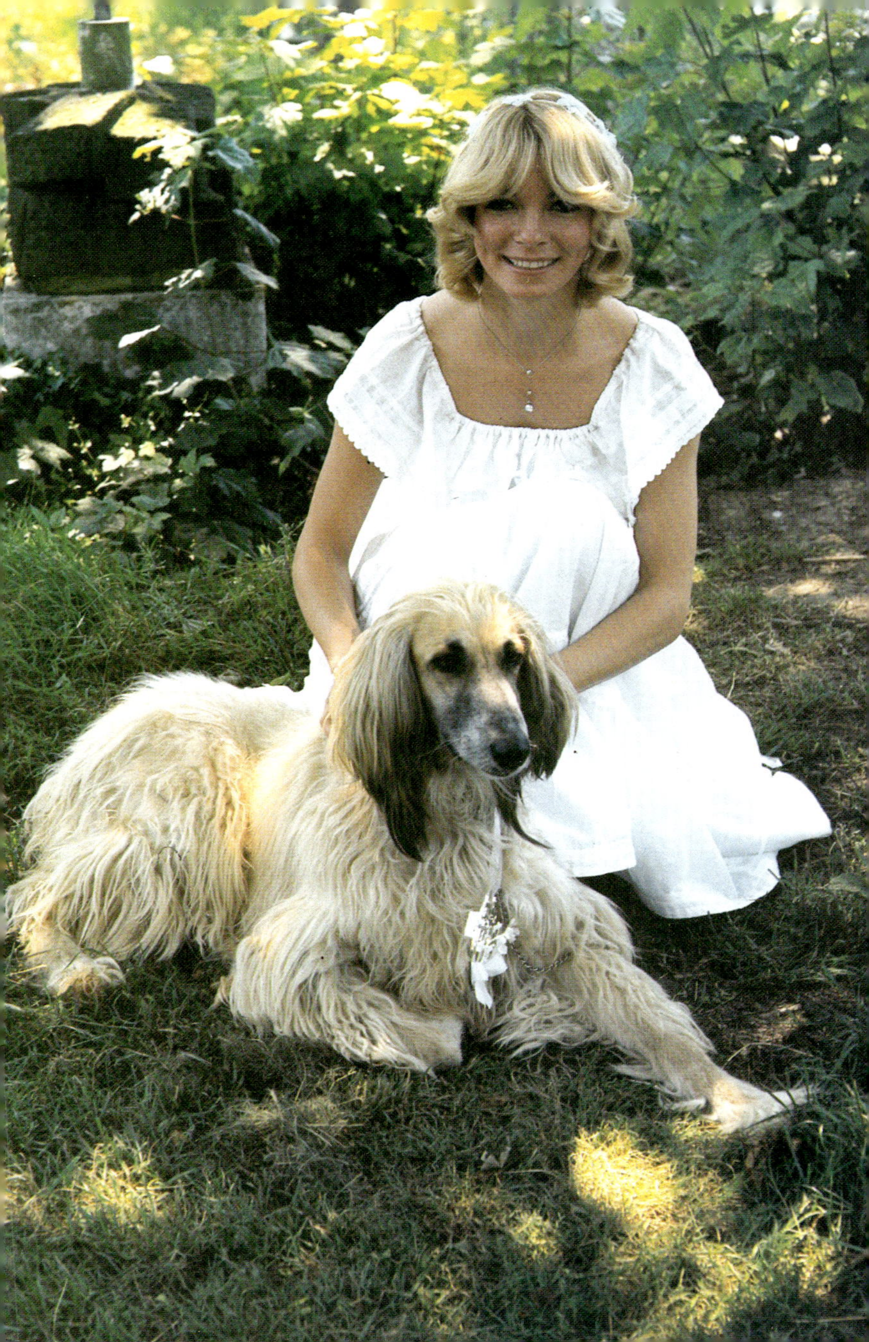

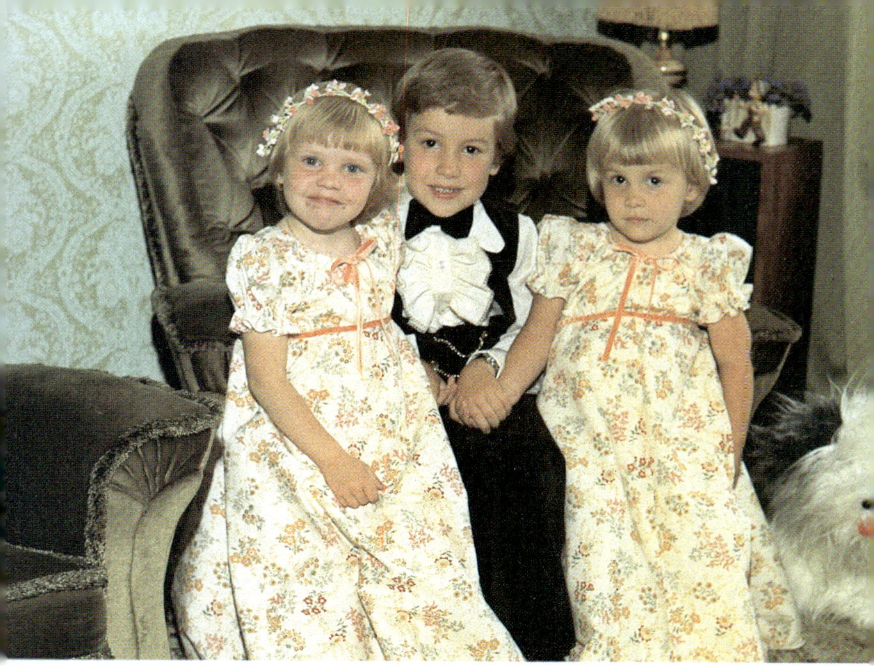

Above. Children always help sell photographs. Any home session should include studies of the attendants and these can often be improved by the addition of a toy mascot. If possible, photograph by daylight – otherwise 'bounce' your electronic flash off the white ceiling.

Previous Page. When an animal is very much part of the family then it is very worthwhile to include at least one photograph in your coverage.

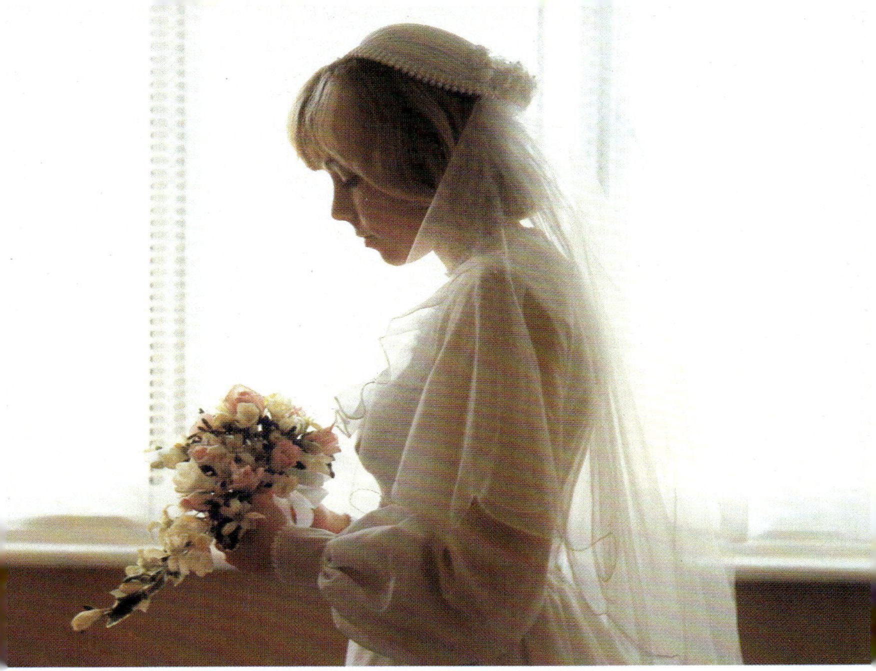

Above. Profiles can be very attractive studies. One method of determining exposure for this type of photograph is to take a reflected or incident reading from the side of the subject's face nearest the camera and then give one stop less exposure. This results in sufficient shadow detail.

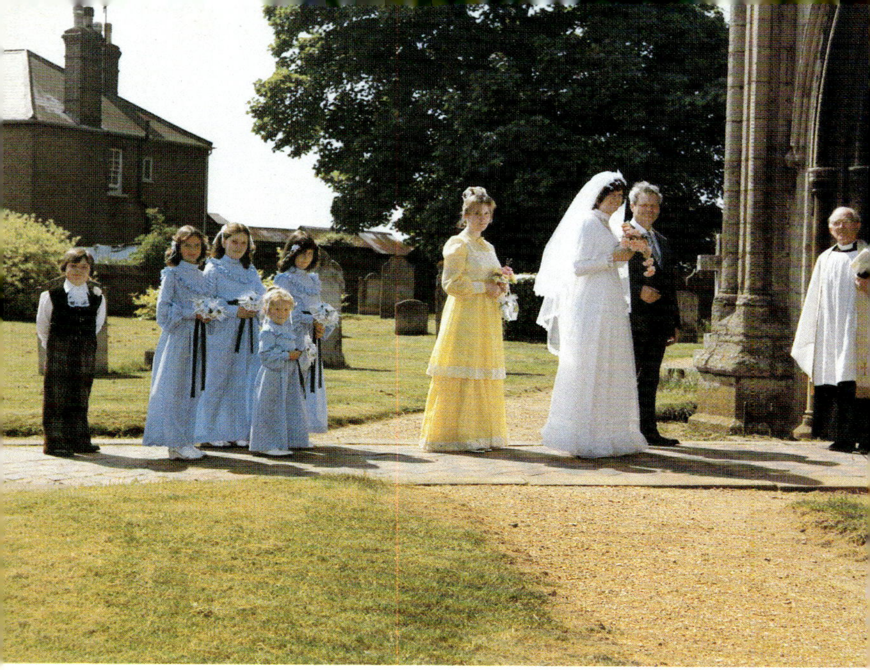

Above. A bridal procession can be an ideal way of showing the bride's arrival at the church door. Try to include the priest with the bride and attendants, and pay special attention to the spacing between people.

Opposite. This is one way to photograph the signing of the register but many alternative arrangements are possible. If the bride has a bouquet then this can be placed on the table in the foreground. Alternative arrangements include the addition of key guests (witnesses) and to have the couple looking towards the camera.

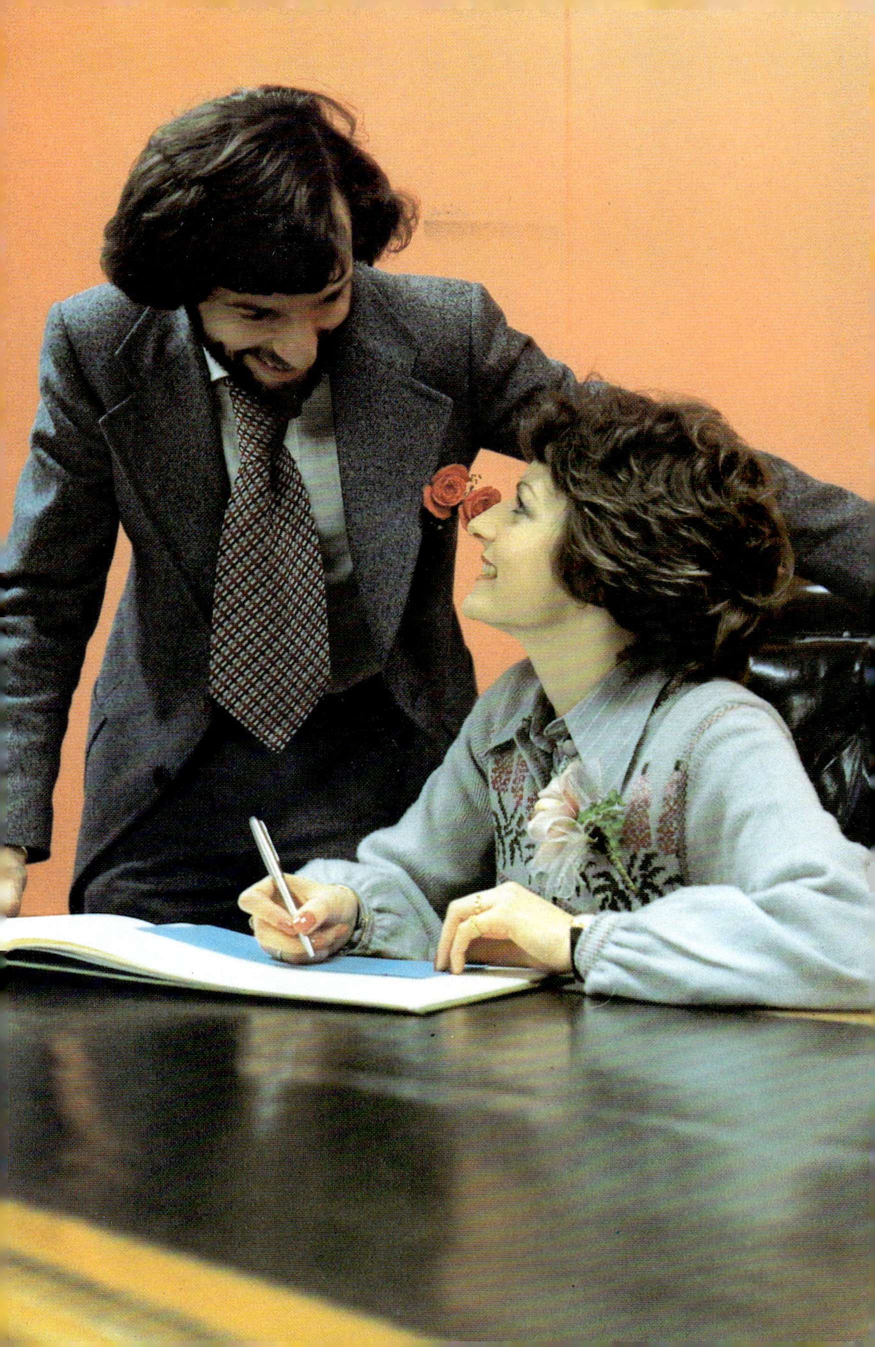

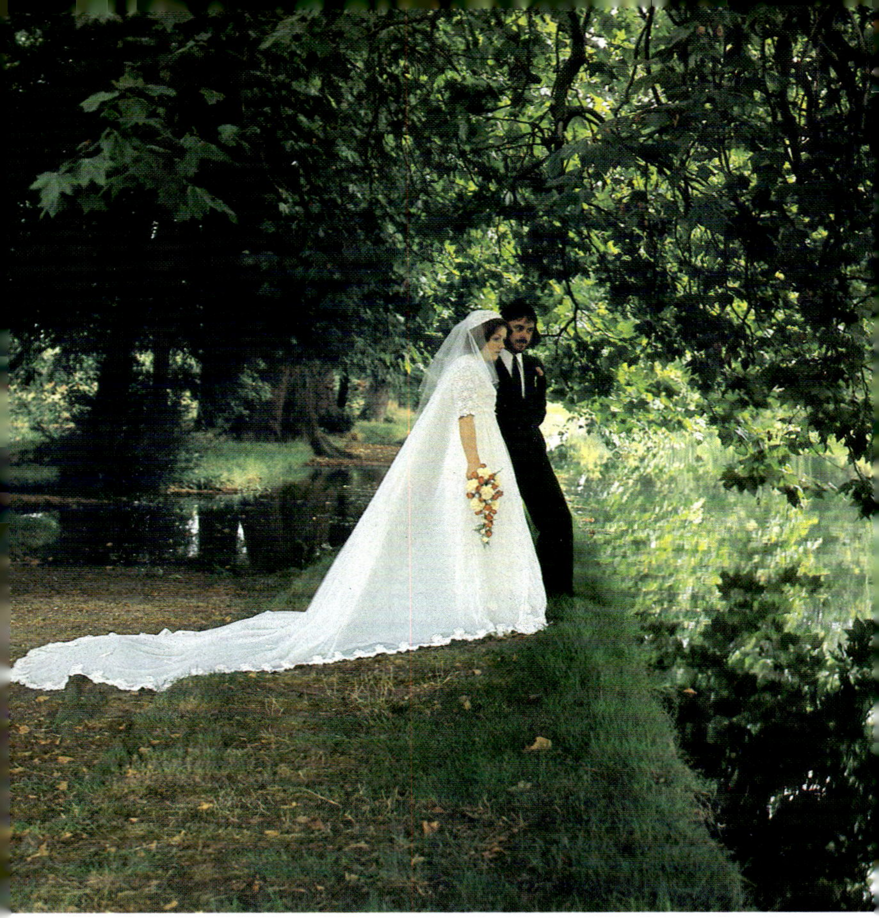

Above. You should make full use of any natural backgrounds to add to the effect of your wedding photographs. A visit to the church and reception venue before the day gives you a chance to locate possible backgrounds.

Opposite. Traditionally the couple framed in the doorway of the church is often very popular. Normally taken with flash to give an evenly lit study, it can be a pleasant change to expose as a semi-silhouette without the use of flash.

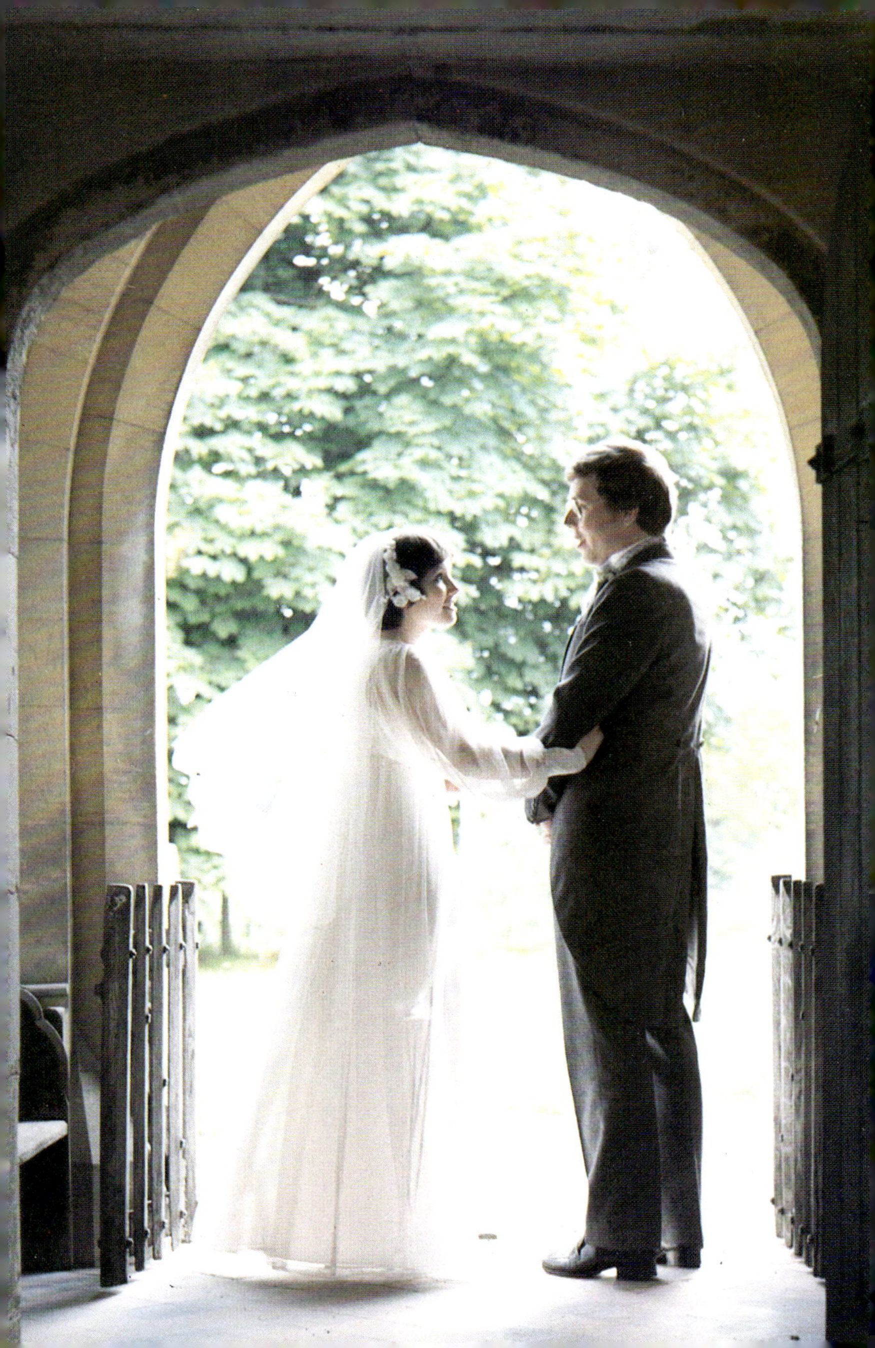

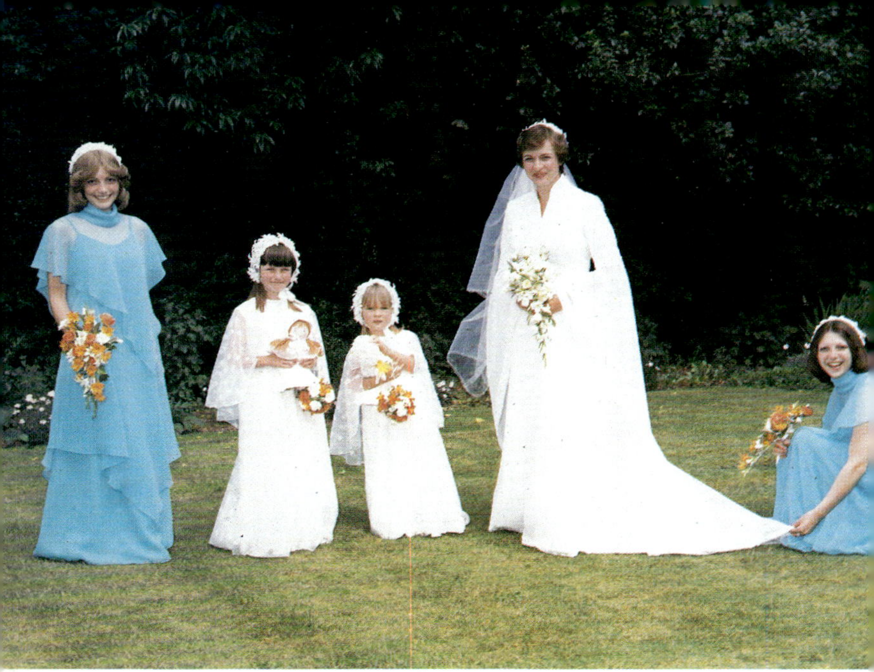

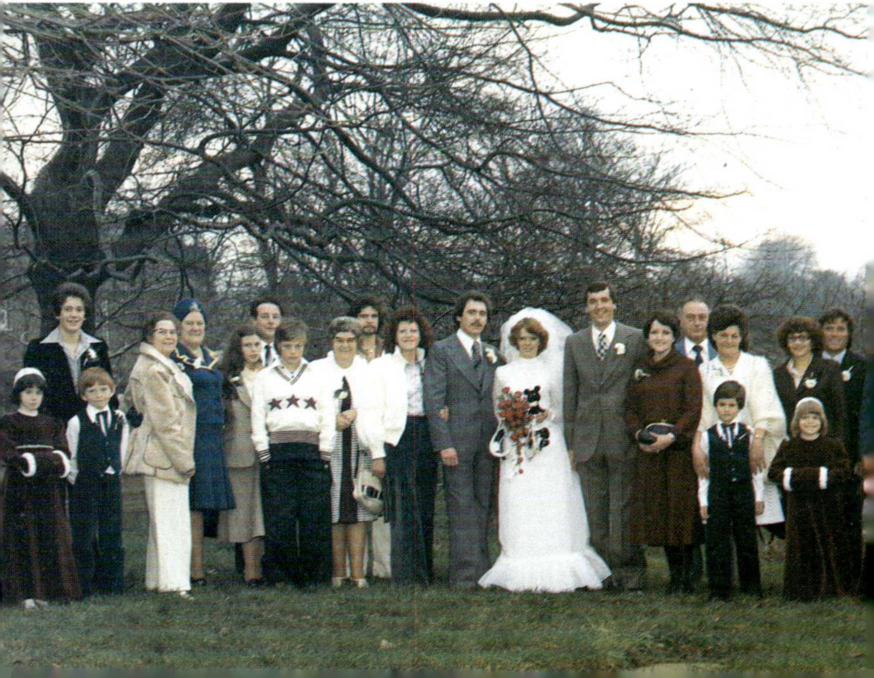

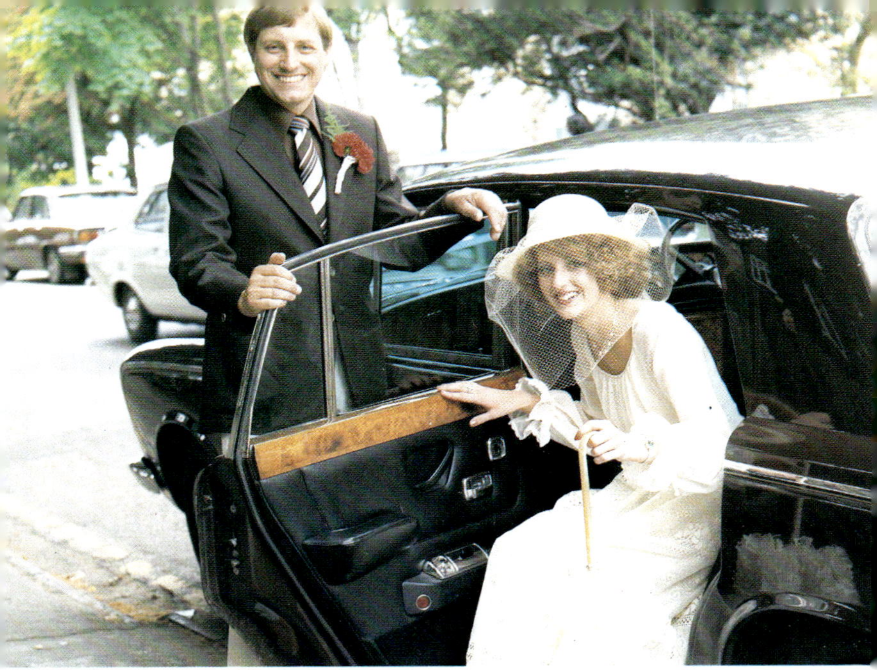

Above. A relaxed informal photograph of the bride arriving for the ceremony.

Opposite, top. The positioning of one bridesmaid to lay out the bride's train helps to add variety and informality to an otherwise rather traditional photograph.

Opposite, bottom. When photographing large groups ensure that everyone can see the camera – arrange the children along the front row or in front of everyone.

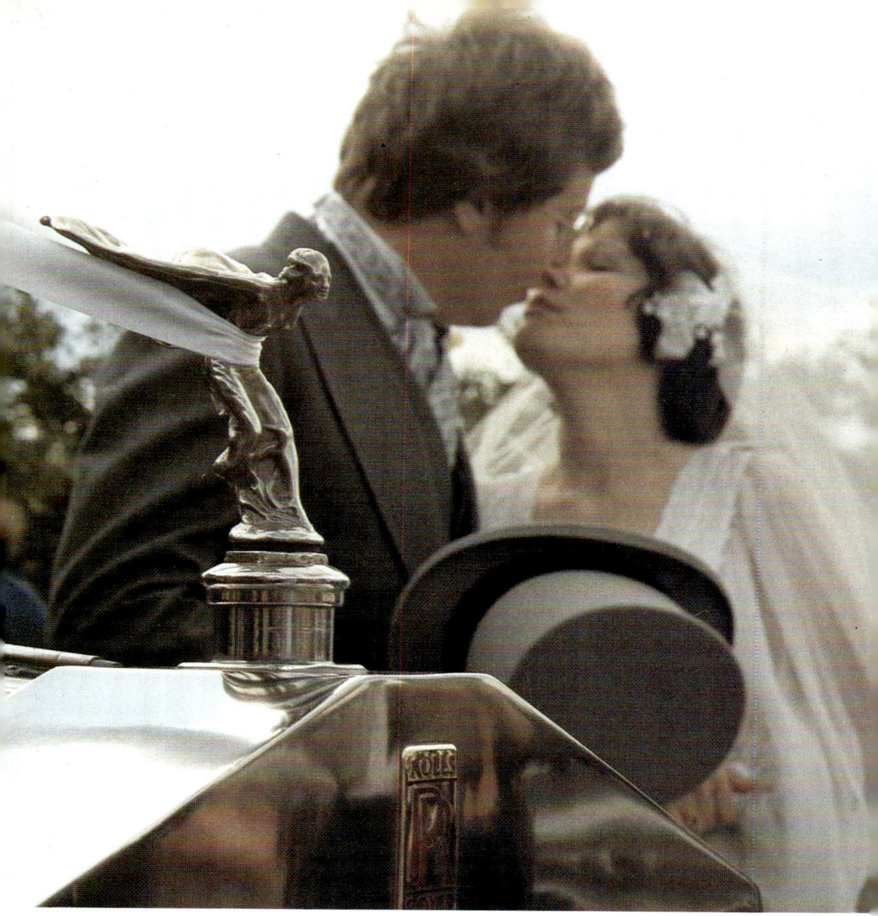

Above. Sharp focusing on the Rolls Royce motif at an aperture of *f* 11 has thrown the embracing couple slightly out of focus. This kind of photograph makes a possible alternative to the more conventional car photograph.

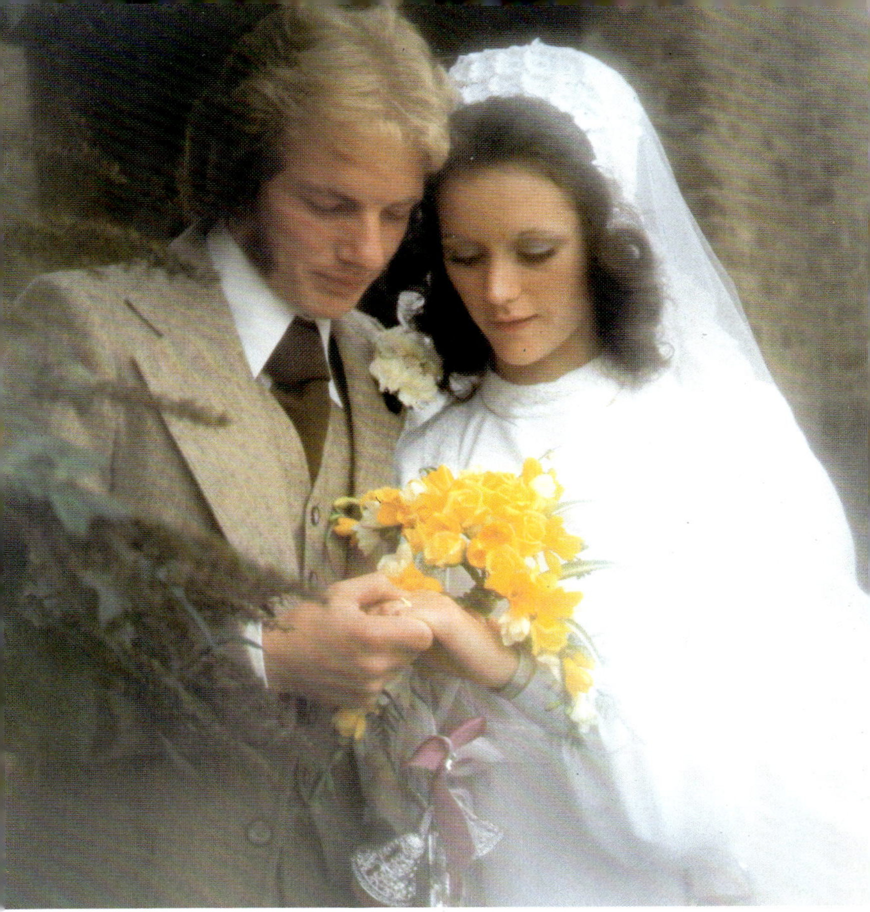

Above. Use of the 'misty' filter heightens the romantic mood of this composition.

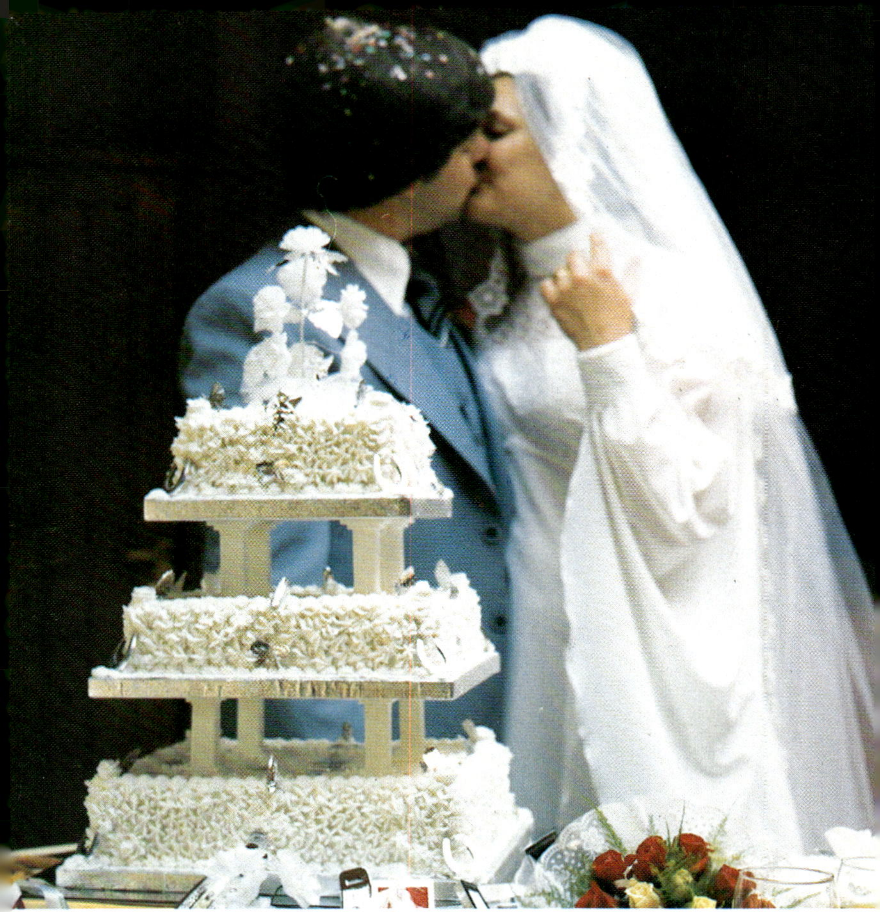

Above. By using an aperture of around *f* 5.6 and focusing sharply on the cake with the couple defocused in the background you can obtain a more pleasing result than the standard cake photograph.

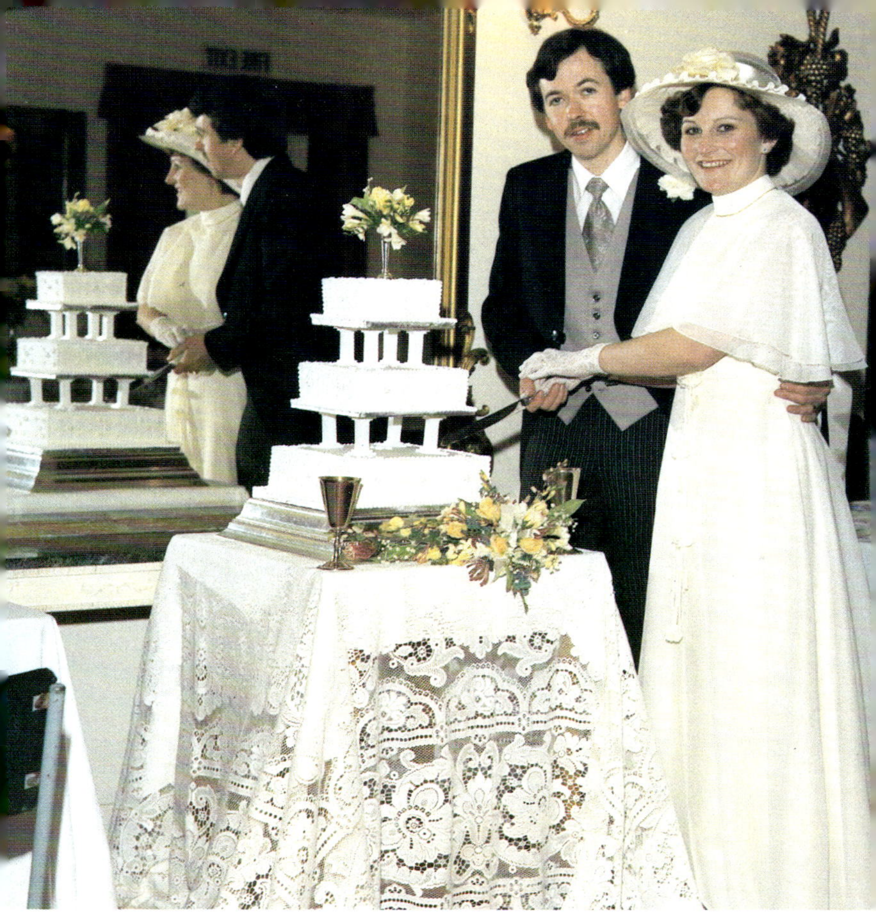

Above. When photographing the cutting of the cake, which is usually posed before it actually happens, you should ensure that the bride's white dress is not hidden behind or near the white cake. A simple solution is to pose the groom just to one side of the cake with the bride next to him and furthest from the cake.

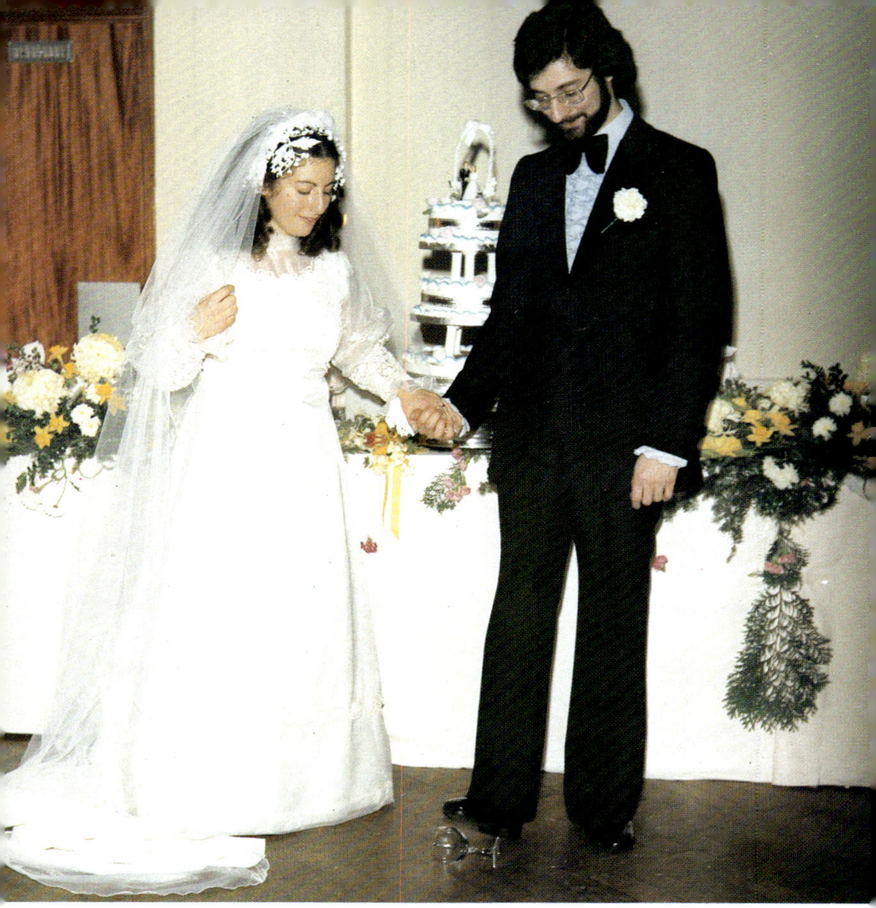

Above. If you can not photograph the traditional Jewish custom of breaking the glass as it happens then you should stage it when you reach the reception.

Opposite, top. When photographing a christening you should always try to capture the precise moment of baptism – sometimes this is not allowed at the actual moment but the priest may allow you to re-enact it later.

Opposite, bottom. When posing sports groups you should aim for some kind of uniformity, such as folded arms or a kneeling front row.

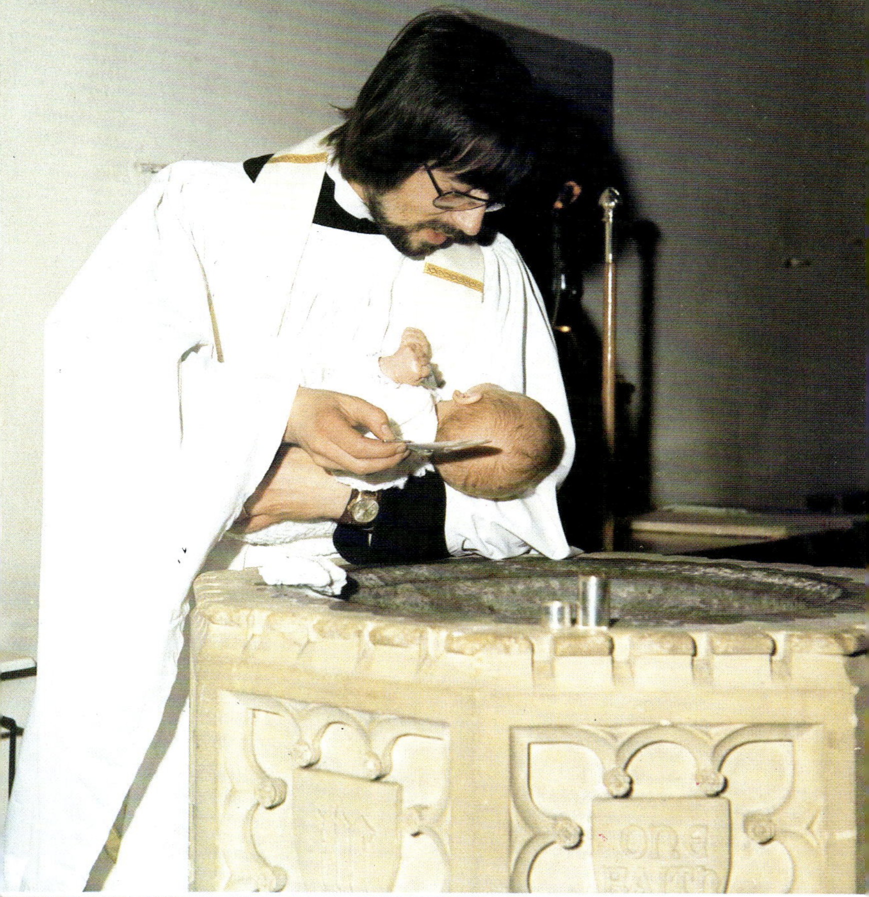

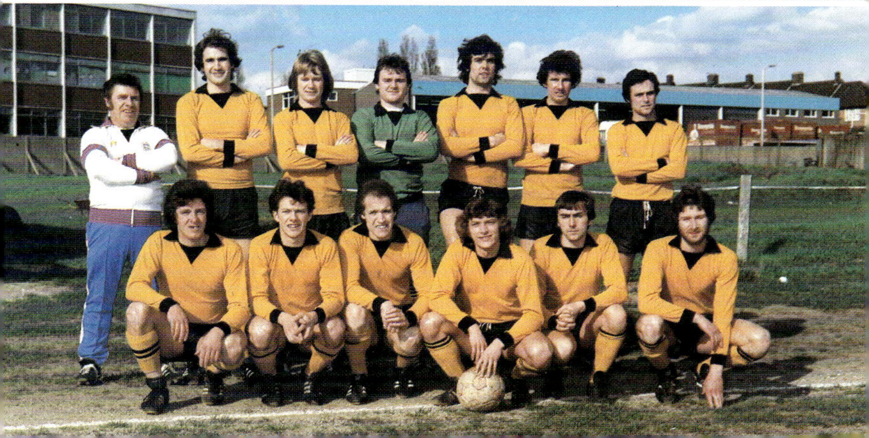

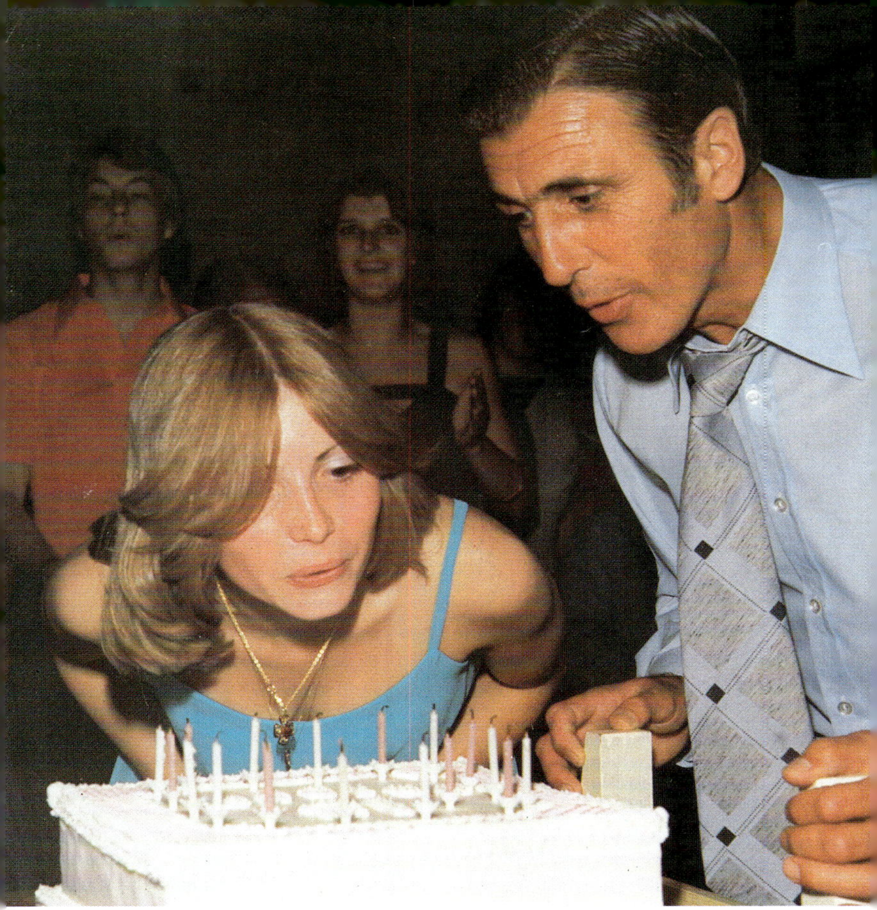

Above. Birthday parties, particularly landmarks such as an 18th birthday, are well worth photographing. Try to include parents whenever possible.

All photographs are by Bob Bluffield.

niture. To make the composition really relaxed it can be very pleasing to pose the bride reclined on the sofa full-length. Of course, you must take great care in posing this type of photograph; otherwise the dress may be damaged. The bride can sit back into a corner of the sofa and place her legs along its length – perhaps with one foot slightly raised to give a bend in her knee. The attendants can be placed behind the sofa with their hands on the back and looking at the bride. Although extremely difficult to arrange and even more difficult to describe in words, if set up tastefully the shot can be successful.
A popular way of photographing the bride with her attendants is to set the dress as you would for the normal full-length bridal portrait. The bridesmaids and page boy are then posed around the bride either as a formal group or spaced carefully to give a 'tidy' casual study.

Attendants

The attendants' photographs have largely been covered above but it can also be worthwhile to take individual portraits of the bridesmaids and page boy especially if the attendants are young children. A pleasant outdoor setting allows you to work at higher shutter speeds than the window shots mentioned already. Aim for full-length portraits because the photographs should emphasize the dresses and outfits the attendants are wearing for the occasion.
Groomsmen and ushers can also be included in certain photographs but these are best done at the church.
Another worthwhile way of picturing the various attendants is to include a portrait of each alone with the bride. This could perhaps be a gentle study of the bride bending low to receive a kiss from the page boy or a bridesmaid admiring the bride's bouquet.

Bride with both parents

It is essential that a good portrait study of the bride with her parents is included in your coverage. Of course advanced planning plays an important part and you should be aware *before* the wedding of the exact situation in the bride's home. Nothing can be worse than a photographer asking for a mum or a dad when the bride does not have one or the other. The parents may be divorced and therefore the photographer is wise to find out before dropping a colossal 'clanger'. If you do not already have the information beforehand, ask the chief bridesmaid or someone who has an intimate knowledge of the family. The same naturally applies when dealing with the bridegroom's family.

This section assumes that both the bride's parents are present at the home when you arrive.

One way of depicting the parents with their daughter which offers a break from the usual sharp close-up is to use controlled depth of field. Take the bride and place her a few feet from the camera position in a three-quarter length, semi-profile pose. Place the parents in the background. Arrange them so that they *look* together and happy. You can try placing the father's left arm around the mother's shoulders while his right hand holds her left hand. Focus on the bride and, by using an aperture of about *f*11 (depending on the distance between bride and her parents and the format that you are using) the bride will be sharp but her parents will be recognizable but slightly out of focus. This particular shot usually goes down very well and emphasizes the family love that exists between the daughter and her watchful parents. The bride is of course the most important person on that day and she is therefore maintained in sharp focus.

A close-up of the parents with their daughter should also be included. It is important to keep the hands of the subjects occupied and this can be achieved by the mother and father both taking hold of their daughter's left hand. You could place both parents on the right of the bride, and take her hand across to them. If the father is tall or of a heavier build than the mother then you should place him in the middle of the small group and stand him behind mother and daughter so that his face can easily be seen but the weight of his body is hidden.

A third method is to take a formal full-length study of the bride with her mother and father. Although in larger homes this can be taken successfully indoors, a suitable outdoor background provides a change from any less formal studies you may have already taken within the house.

Bride with close family

To save time after the wedding ceremony it may be better to take a family group at the bride's home if all members of the immediate family are present.

Close family includes mother, father, the bride, her brothers and sisters and their respective husbands, wives and children. Do not forget that in many homes the pet cat, dog or even horse may need to be included.

Indoors, try posing the bride in an easy chair and arrange the family, assuming there are not too many, around the backs and sides. Take care however not to lose the bride in the crowd and not place her so low in a chair that she looks like a dwarf.

Similarly the bride and her parents can be seated on higher chairs such as those used around the dining room table. The brothers and sisters can then be placed standing at the backs of the chairs with any small children seated on the floor.

When the bride has only one brother or a sister, it can be a pleasant touch to take the pair as a close-up portrait study. Once more the window area can be used to good effect.

The bride may be very close to the family pet. Be sure to ask her if she wants a portrait taken with the family cat or other domestic animal. If the pet is sufficiently inactive use the available daylight near the window; if not try bounced flash.

The main family groups are taken after the ceremony so there is no need to photograph any aunts and uncles that may be waiting at the bride's home.

It is wise to include a close group of the grandparents if they are present. This saves time later on especially as senior citizens are rather slow on their feet and may feel reluctant because of this to take part in a photograph at the church.

Bride leaving home

As you should be at the wedding ceremony in time for the arrival of the bride, stage this shot when the remainder of the 'home' session is completed.

Take the bride out onto the front path leading from the house. Her

father is posed with his hand on the doorhandle of the almost closed door. Although obviously staged, the composition does emphasize the fact that the bride and her father are leaving the house.
Some bridal gowns have hooks so that the bride can lift the train and carry the dress as she walks. The bride should be holding this or have the train draped over one arm. This makes the pose look more natural. If you have the chance of framing the composition with a branch or two from a tree in the garden or can shoot through an array of coloured flower blooms, do so. This will make your photograph stand out that much more.

Conclusions to the home session

Some basic ideas that can be used at the bride's home have been mentioned. The type of wedding, the people you are dealing with and the home backgrounds all play an important part. If there is a happy home atmosphere then it is up to you to bring this point out in the mood of the photographs you take. This is easier to achieve than it sounds but a happy situation affects the way you work.
Frequently when working on the home session you will have to adapt to tight surroundings. Choose your rooms for working carefully. If the bride's parents' bedroom is better suited for your purposes than her own room then ask to use that. Override any objections about using a particular room in a pleasant and tactful manner.
Wedding households are usually frantic. Do not become put off by this atmosphere but go along with it, and try to remain calm yourself. Aunts, uncles and all and sundry are often visitors to the bride's home prior to the ceremony. Ask guests to move from any room that you may wish to use, although try not to upset the household unduly.
If you do your job well then the home session will be appreciated by the bride, her family and of course the bridegroom. After all, this set of photographs portrays a part of the marriage which the groom has not had the chance to see.

Traditional versus casual

In the home session many photographers opt to take the majority of their photographs by available daylight. The casual, softly lit and misty images of the bride should be taken to blend carefully with the formal group photographs which will be taken immediately after the ceremony.

There is nothing radically wrong with taking all of your photographs in the traditional mode but they will look stereotyped. The casual approach lends a certain amount of creative licence that can allow any good wedding operator to demonstrate his talents to advantage. Weddings do not have to be stiff and starchy. The couple has life, so too have their guests. Therefore it is important that you try to show it.

If you find a different way to stage a standard pose then try it. If you think it may not work still give it a try but do the traditional shot as well. Then compare the two studies and see which you think is best. The chances are that the casual version will win.

Your approach to the casual method can be decided by judging the available daylight that can be used. If it is soft and even, then try to work it into a shot as much as possible without the need to resort to flash. If you want a little artificial light, then bounce just a little as fill-in from the ceiling. Do not overdo the lighting so that the result is bleached and overexposed. The easy way is to use flash as the main lighting throughout but your photographs will be no more than record shots. The beauty and feelings of the bride and her family will be captured in a more gentle and convincing manner if photographed by natural light.

With the close family groups, try to bring in pleasant and cosy corners of the family house. Pose your subjects in a casual manner rather than in the formal way that you will probably use later on for the large groups. A casual approach at the home session helps the bride to be more relaxed when the ceremony stage is reached.

A good photographer is a versatile one. Learn to deal with each aspect of the wedding situation in various ways and you will always have a card up your sleeve that can be used for effect or to add a little extra to a standard pose.

The Western Church Ceremony

Having completed the 'home' session with the bride the

photographer must now move on to the Church for coverage of the wedding ceremony. It is important to arrive with enough time in hand to photograph the arrival of the wedding guests before embarking on the major task of covering the marriage service itself.

Guest arrivals

The guests are usually at the church before the parents or the couple. There are two main ways of photographing them as they arrive: the 'walking' shots, and posed shots. The posed variety does give the photographer greater control because he is able to place his subjects in the desired location and stance. This is not to say that the mobile variety are any less popular; and they do have greater candid appeal because they are 'snapped' as the guests walk down the path to the church.

If you prefer to shoot the 'walking' pictures find a suitable spot where you aim to capture your subjects. Either pre-focus and use as much depth of field as possible (i.e. small apertures such as *f*16) or wander about with a hand-held camera covering guests at different points of the path as they approach. The latter method will possible result in photographs that have more life and appeal.

The 'walking' arrivals

Unless the couple has requested this type of coverage the selling potential of these photographs can be very limited. This is hardly surprising when you examine some of the pictures taken in this way. Many show no imagination (albeit difficult to add sparkle to this type of shot!) and it is not uncommon to find large numbers of 'walking' poses which are out of focus.

If you do intend to take these photographs and they are specifically for the couple, try to vary the viewpoint and the backgrounds. Get as close as you can and whenever possible try to add just a little bit of thought to your work. For example, picture couples coming through the lychgate of the church or maybe walking beneath a framework of overhanging branches. Even a few taken with the misty attachment can make a vast difference.

Posed arrivals

Some guests may prefer to be portrayed full-length as this shows off the lady's outfit or the man's suit. Select a couple of pleasant backgrounds, if any are suitable, and alternate between them. As the guests come through the gate of the church take them aside and place them against the background you have chosen. Speed is very important and this is one of the reasons that guest arrivals can be a useful way for a novice to begin wedding coverage as it gives practise in handling and posing people at speed.

Always ensure that there are no gaps between legs and turn the subjects in towards each other. Ask them to move the leg nearer the camera a fraction forward. The man can place his arm around the lady's waist or his hand on the back of her elbow. Arms round partners shoulders can look cramped and may also bunch up the man's suit. Posing the subjects in this manner is easy once the basic method is grasped and makes each person appear as elegant as possible in the photographs.

Do not be afraid to move a person's hand, leg or foot. It is often much easier to guide the subject into a pose rather than try verbal explanations that are usually difficult to follow.

Finally, the subjects should be smiling, the men's jackets should be buttoned (if they do not wear a waistcoat) and women's handbags should be placed tidily on the wrist or shoulder nearest the camera.

The groom's arrival

You must not forget to take a picture or two of the bridegroom and his best man when they reach the church. Some photographers, especially in the USA, visit the groom at home in much the same way as they would the bride. If that is the case then a couple of photographs can be taken of the groom with his parents, with the best man and preparing himself for the wedding. However few photographers include this part of the coverage in the UK although if time permits it would be a pleasant touch.

If you do want to try a session at the groom's home perhaps take a shot of him looking into the mirror putting on his tie. Another could be included of his mother putting on his buttonhole flower, with father looking on. Lastly, take a shot of the bridegroom with the best man just about to get into the car, or of them taking a swift drink in a nearby bar to steady their nerves before the ceremony. If you indulge in this coverage be sure not to delay the groom from getting to the ceremony because it is of great importance that he arrives before his bride.

As for the arrival photographs, the same mundane shot showing the groom being dragged by the best man over the church threshold is often still taken. There is no harm in portraying the groom and best man in an informal pose but there are better ways of doing so.

If there is an attractive gate or wooden fence nearby then it can make a pleasant composition to place the groom and his best man behind it so that they are leaning on it in a relaxed fashion. Frame tightly and have them looking towards the camera with happy expressions. The composition is simple but it never fails to sell.

The groom can be given the same informal treatment for close-up portraits, to give a composition which will be greatly appreciated by the bride.

If you wish to keep your shooting formal, the favourite way is simply to photograph the groom and his best man shaking hands in the church doorway. A three-quarter-length pose is best suited if the two men are of similar height. Marked height differences require the camera to be taken further away and you will therefore need to take a full-length study.

Once the bridegroom and his best man have been ushered away into the church your attention now turns to cover the bride's arrival.

The bride's arrival

At most church weddings the bride arrives with her father or whoever else may be 'giving her away'. There is no ruling about who gives the bride's hand to the groom in marriage, but traditionally it is her father.

If the bride arrives in a roomy limousine a nice composition can be achieved by removing her father from the car, placing him half in and half out of the vehicle with the door open. The photographer

A

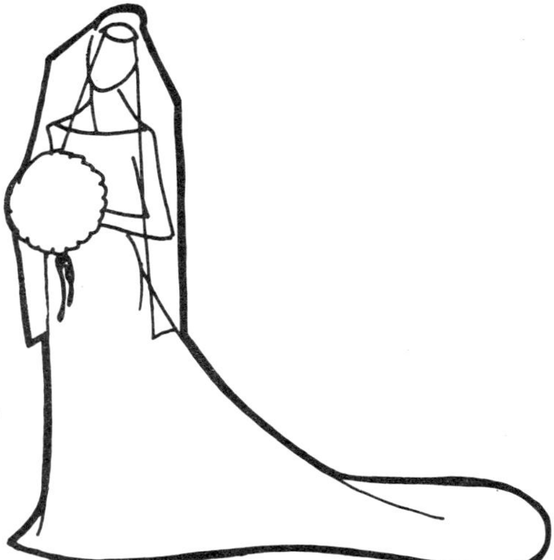

B

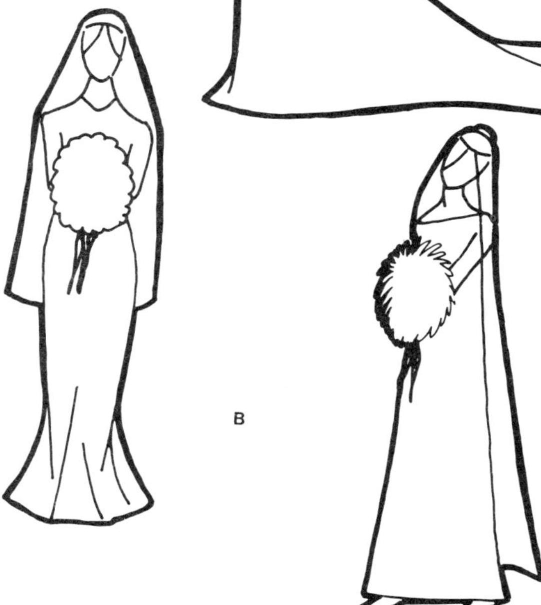

The bride full-length. A. The bride's gown must be displayed to its very best. Arrange the gown so that it flows out and ask her to move forward slightly. The bride should swing towards the camera but from the waist only. B. Avoid flat-on frontal studies because they tend to look unglamorous, but instead pose your subject at an angle to the camera.

should obviously shoot his composition on the kerbside of the road. The father is shown leaning into the car and holding his daughter's hand as if he is about to help her from her seat. The pair can either be looking at the camera or, better still, at each other. Ensure that the expressions show happiness. If enough daylight exists to allow sufficient depth of field for the purpose, expose without flash. If not then try to bounce it from the inside of the car roof.

It is usual to include a photograph of the bride as she steps from her car. The success of this shot depends largely on the type of car being used. You may have to take the bride out of the car and then reposition her on the edge of the seat. One hand should hold her bouquet while the other is placed on the car door. Take care with the composition to ensure it captures the right moment. There is no harm in adding the bride's father or the chauffeur holding open the car door. If the sun plays shadows on the bride's face it may be necessary to use a little fill-in flash in order to give the composition lift (see chapter on Technique and Equipment).

The bride may arrive with her veil covering her face. It is preferable to take your photographs with the veil removed so that the bride's features can clearly be seen. However, you may find that she does not want to have the veil lifted. If this proves to be the case then do not persist; take your photograph regardless. In any case, the veil will probably be covering the bride's face for the next shot which shows the bridal party at the church door.

If the bride arrives in a veteran, vintage or other car of special interest, then she should be pictured with her father in a full-length study of the car. With open-topped cars father and daughter may be photographed seated; an especially good composition if the car driver is dressed in period costume. Similarly, father can be taken giving a helping 'lift down' of his daughter from older cars which are high off the ground. Whatever method you use to portray this subject, you will find that old cars do help to sell photographs.

It is worth photographing the bride's attendants as a small group when they get to the church. When the bride arrives, take the attendants from wherever they may be waiting and set up the procession. The bride's father should be on her left arm (reverse in the USA) and the attendants can be placed behind them in pairs, or singly, as you prefer. Form the procession so that it looks as if they are walking

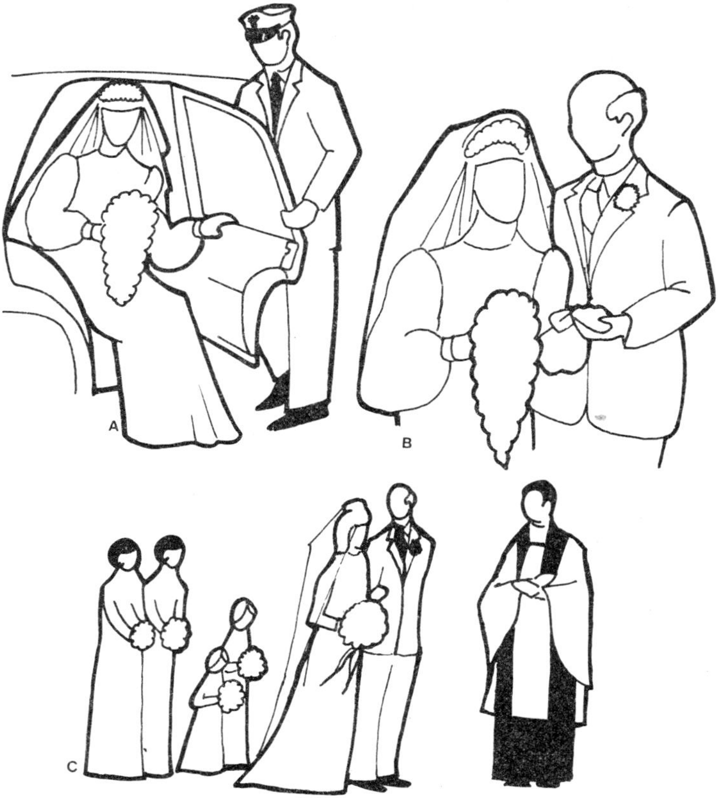

The bride arriving for the wedding. A. Take time to carefully position the bride as she leaves the car and if necessary re-seat her so that she looks comfortable. Her father or the chauffeur can also be included in the composition. B. The bride and father should be angled slightly towards each other and you should pay special attention to the position of the hands. C. If the church entrance is attractive then try a 'processional' photograph of the bride with her father and attendants, and if possible, include the priest. Always take this shot from the bride's side.

towards the church door but take care to set those nearest to the camera a foot or two back so that everyone appearing in the picture can be seen. If the priest is cooperative ask him to stand on the threshold of the church to welcome the party as they arrive.

If there is a shortage of space outside the church a procession photograph may still be possible by shooting a 'looking back' composition. Place the bride on her father's arm as before and pair off the bridesmaids and page boys so that they taper outwards towards the camera. This permits everyone to be seen.

If you have a chance and the priest has no objections, you may also be able to take a shot or two as the bridal party await the appropriate moment to walk up the aisle. Because the inside of church doorways are frequently dark, flash is almost certainly to be required especially if you really do want to take 'grab shots' capturing the subjects unawares.

Once the bridal party are in the church you can proceed to take whatever shots the priest has granted permission for during the religious ceremony.

The ceremony

By using tact, it is up to you to encourage the church authorities you deal with to allow you to photograph the religious parts of the wedding. Firstly, always make the point of taking any ceremony photographs (apart from the signing of the register and the couple walking back along the aisle) without the aid of flash. Also ensure that you certainly do not intrude upon the ceremony in any way during the course of your photography.

If you have permission to take photographs during the service, avoid covering every point in the ceremony. A few well-composed pictures will be better received than a large number which do not convey very much.

If possible, work from a tripod, as you need a very slow shutter speed. With a hand-held camera, in order to opt for the fastest possible speed you must often have your lens set at maximum aperture.

The basic list of subjects is as follows:

Bride and bridegroom at the altar – view from back of church
Exchange of rings
View from balcony
Communion, etc.
Couple signing register
Couple walking back up aisle
Couple in church doorway

These eight main subjects have a few variations but do not overdo things. Three or four photographs are normally sufficient unless the couple and their families are especially religious.

Bride and bridegroom at altar

You may feel that it is inappropriate to photograph the couple while they are praying because of the disturbance it might cause. If you intend shooting from the front of the church then this is likely to be true; you could intrude upon the sensitivity of the service. However, there is nothing wrong in shooting from the back of the church where you will not be noticed unless your camera shutter is especially noisy.

If you wish to include this shot ask the bridesmaids before the service to stand aside when they reach the foot of the aisle. The shot can be made more attractive if taken very low to the floor. When the church has a smooth, uncarpeted floor this sometimes appears glass-like in photographs and can give attractive reflections. The low angle also encompasses the ends of the pews and leads the viewers' eyes to the central figures (the couple) in the photograph. Aim also to include the stained glass window above the altar when there is one.

The bride and groom at prayer can also be captured from a side aisle from a viewpoint a little way behind the bride so that you can include her train if it is flowing behind her.

Some priests like couples to face the congregation during all or part of the marriage. This makes long shots even more significant. It also, of course, makes framing some of the other shots somewhat different.

Take your light reading from the camera position but do not be afraid to use relatively long exposures (up to one second). There are points during the ceremony when the congregation is almost motionless. This allows you to capture available-light photographs even under the extremes of poor lighting typical of church interiors. In these situations the faster 400 ASA films are ideal, and are capable of producing excellent enlargements. The misty attachment may add a little lift to the interior photographs. However, do not shoot all of them misty because this kills the novelty. One, possibly two ceremony shots are enough.

Exchange of rings

If you have been granted permission to cover the exchange of rings you need to find a suitable, unobtrusive spot near the altar. You may have to 'hide' behind a screen or a row of pews in a side chapel. Aim to shoot from the groom's side of the church so that the bride's face can be seen when the groom places the ring on her finger.
A quick 'burst' of flash at this point would certainly destroy the atmosphere and this is why you should aim to take your interior photographs by available light.
There are other key points in wedding services, they vary from religion to religion and from denomination to denomination. These points should (permission providing) form part of your coverage.

View from the balcony

A number of churches have a balcony either at the back or, in fewer cases, running down one or both sides of the church. Watch your suit however, because balaconies are usually forgotten by the cleaners and are therefore dust traps!
If you do not bother with the rear view shot from ground floor level it can make a change to take it from the balcony. A starburst attachment (already described) may give a nice touch by picking up any light points such as the flames of any candles on the altar.
A side balcony may give you a better view for taking the ring shots, but it is best to try and check this beforehand. Always ensure that

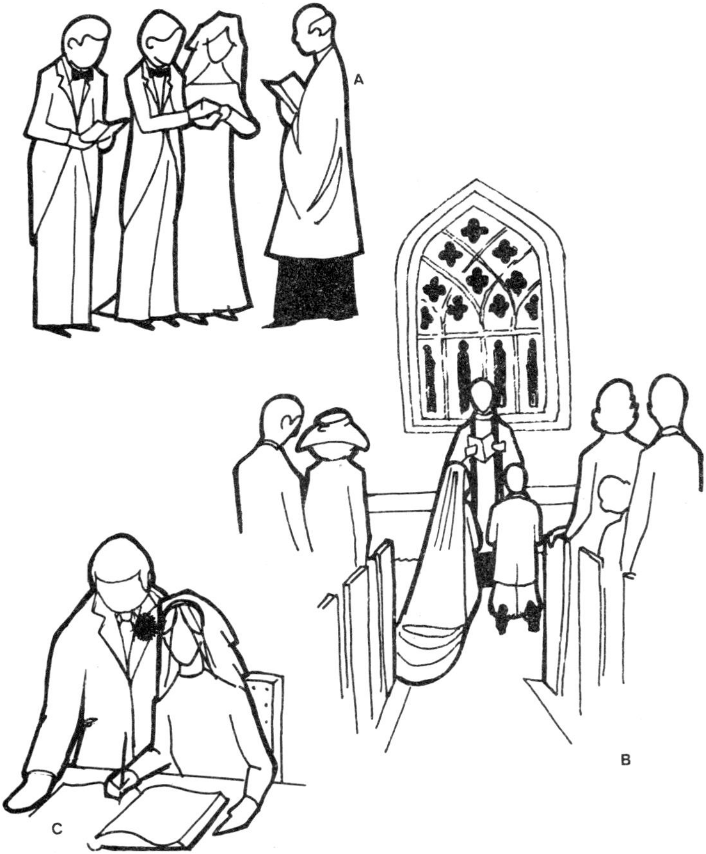

The ceremony. A. Use available light to capture the placing of the rings and photograph from the groom's side to ensure that the bride's face is visible. B. A low-angle shot from the back of the church when the couple are kneeling makes an attractive composition. C. A good method of arranging the register-signing photograph is to have the groom standing and the bride seated. The groom should have one hand on the back of the chair and the other on the table; he should also be leaning slightly forward.

the person conducting the service has no objections to you using the balcony.

Communion

If the couple are Roman Catholic or belong to a high church, their service may include Holy Communion. Be sure to include this in your coverage at the time when the priest gives the chalice of wine to the bride or groom. This is one point when you may need flash because the movements are quite rapid.

Couple signing register

This is one of the photographs which ought to be included. Rarely you may find a priest who is not willing to allow you into the vestry for the signing.

If you have not taken any photographs during the course of the service, then the shots of the signing of the register are of great importance because they are the very first photographs of the couple as husband and wife.

The majority of registers are signed in the vestry at the end of the service. Be warned, however, that his is not always the case. Sometimes the priest will hold up the ceremony after the marriage vows have been made and the register is then signed either in the church or the vestry. A wide-angle lens can be handy, but if you use one, make sure that your flash can illuminate the whole area covered by the lens.

The best way to portray the occasion is to place the bride in a chair with the pen in her hand and the register before her. If she has a floral bouquet then put this in the foreground, on the table. The groom should stand to her right but slightly behind the chair. His left hand can be placed on the chair back while he leans forward onto his right hand which is on the table. This brings their heads fairly close to enable you to take a tidy composition.

There are other ways to take this. One pose is to have the couple looking towards the camera, in another you might turn their heads towards the register or perhaps each other. If a misty filter is added to the latter it can look very pleasant.

If there is sufficient room, you can take another mini-group photograph adding the two witnesses, possibly the parents and the bride's attendants and priest.
Another close-up may be taken to show the priest handing the couple the marriage certificate. He may well appreciate this gesture and it will help establish you in his 'good books' if you send him a print!
It is normal for the photographs to be staged *after* the actual signing has been completed. The main reason for this is that it is easier for the registrar to complete everything swiftly without having to move into the correct position for the photographer.
If the signing takes place during the service rather than at the end of it, the same rules generally apply. Flash, of course, is often required unless the couple are evenly lit from light entering from a window. When no table is available for posing the shot, it sometimes needs to be set up on a shelf or window ledge in a corner or to one side of the vestry. This is always a difficult composition and you can only arrange this shot as you see it. The rule is to have the bride placed nearer to the camera than the groom unless she is markedly taller or broader than he.

Couple walking back up aisle

This is one of the most difficult of all the wedding photographs to take. The couple are in a position where the photographer has less control than at any other time. At the point of firing the shutter the bride's face may be turned to look at one of the guests or the couple could be looking at each other. No matter what, the composition can be awkward.
Of course the photographer could take control and stop the couple at a suitable point on the aisle, but this defeats the whole object of a 'walking' shot and the end result always looks stationary.
You therefore need to prefocus on a set point 3–5 m (10–15 ft) from the camera and fire the shutter when the couple reach this point. However, as if by fate, it is often at this moment that the couple turn their heads away.
The aisle photograph needs to be sharp and also to register some of the background. Thus, to avoid the detail in the background from

turning black, you need a shutter speed of about 1/30 second with an aperture of *f*8 or *f*11 to allow plenty of depth of field. A slower shutter speed can result in movement blur even with flash to 'freeze' the action. You usually need to set your flash a stop up on the lens setting. If your lens is at *f*8 then you should set the flash at *f*11 and although some overexposing does occur it is not drastic and can be compensated for by the printer. The reason for doing this is to capture the faces of people walking behind the couple rather than leaving them dark as would occur if the correct flash setting was used. When you take the aisle shot make sure that your flash is switched on, that you have wound on your film and have prefocused. This may sound like commonsense but it is amazing how often a photographer can come unstuck during his 'dash' from the vestry to the top of the aisle.

Viewpoint is often a matter of taste, but if you photograph from the back of the aisle this allows you to stand quickly aside and be in a suitable position to arrange the couple for the next shot of them, in the doorway. However, you can often find a better composition by coming to the altar end of the aisle. The altar and chancel can form a very colourful backdrop.

You obviously have to work very fast on this shot and there is usually no second chance should you fail on the first. Watch that your flash sync lead has not fallen out during your progress from the vestry. This is a main factor resulting in the non-firing of electronic flashes!

Couple in church doorway

This can be one of the most attractive shots of the couple and one of your best sellers. Stop the couple as they reach the outer threshold of the church so that they are immediately within the arch of the doorway. Take a few seconds to ensure that the bride's gown is flowing freely behind her and take the opportunity to make a quick light reading. This enables two possibilities to be included, the first lit by flash, the second as a semi-silhouette taken by available light. Separate the couple a little so that they can hold hands rather than link arms. Their backs should be towards the camera and they

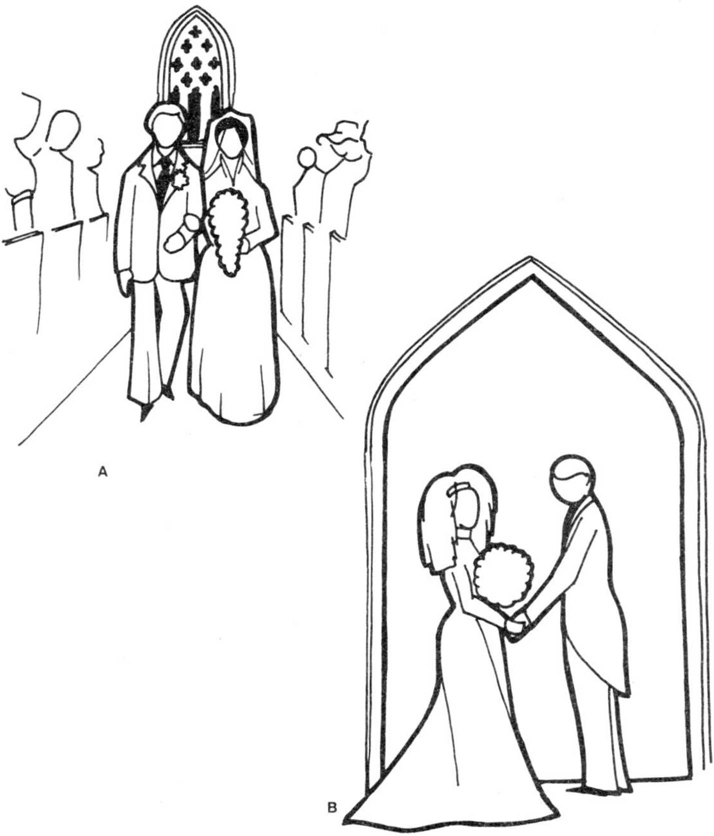

A

B

Coming down the aisle. A. The aisle shot requires flash at about *f*8 or *f*11 to give sufficient depth of field and a shutter speed of about 1/30 second to ensure some background detail is recorded. You should pre-focus shot for about 3 m (10 ft). B. Church doors make pleasant frames. You should stop the couple just inside the doorway an ask them to turn their heads towards the camera.

should be asked to look back over their shoulders towards the camera. The bride should look over her right shoulder, the groom over his left (assuming the groom is on the right of his bride). The bride's floral arrangement should be in her left hand and this should be turned so that it faces the camera. For a correct exposure you should aim to have the outside of the church in correct balance with the interior. Depending on the brightness of the day select your shutter speed accordingly (ensuring you are on a suitable speed for flash if your camera has a focal plane shutter). Your flash should be set at full power if it is computerized so that the sensor does not record a false reading and cut the power output too soon. Full power will avoid the sensor reacting to any part of the church doorway or wall situated between the subjects and the camera.

The couple can either be turned so that their heads look toward the camera or they can look at each other.

The other way is to shoot by available light but this can be difficult because you need to try to take a semi-silhouetted shot without burning out the exterior background too much. On an average day a combination of 1/30 second at *f*5.6 tends to work out about right with 100 ASA colour film.

The couple should be turned to face each other for this photograph. The bride's gown should still be set out behind her, their arms can be brought higher to enable them to embrace. Their heads should be turned to look at each other.

In general younger people tend to favour the moody available-light rendering; the parents and older guests favour the evenly lit flash version.

Even if you take both views you must be able to complete the job in a few seconds; otherwise you will block the guests' exit from the church.

After the Ceremony

This is the busiest period for the wedding photographer. The traditional and informal studies of the couple and their guests must be covered. There are endless possible variations but only the main subjects that must be included have been listed. The informal variations are discussed later on. The following are therefore regarded by couples and their families as 'standards', which any capable wedding photographer must be able to include.

Bride and groom full-length
Bride and groom close-up
Bride and groom with bridesmaids, bride's father and best man (*bridal group*)
Bride and groom with parents
Bride and groom withn close families
Bride and groom with relations
Bride and groom with friends
Bride with bridesmaids
Bridegroom with his parents
Bride and groom with grandparents

The compositions above form the backbone of the wedding day 'story' although by no means should the list be used on its own. Every wedding should be handled by the photographer carefully blending the traditional studies with his own creative compositions mentioned later.

In the USA, it is common for the formal photographs to be taken at the reception rather than immediately following the ceremony. UK weddings are often staged in simpler surroundings and the majority of receptions have neither external grounds or internal space where large groups can be arranged. It is naturally easier to complete the coverage outside the church or registry office.

Bride and groom – full-length

Once the couple have come out of the church you should be at their side ready to direct them to wherever you have decided to shoot your photographs.

Church doors should be avoided unless there is no other suitable background or, the church doorway is particularly attractive and forms a good backdrop.

In English weddings the bridegroom must *always* stand on the right of his bride. At Jewish weddings and American weddings it is the opposite. This is tradition, and according to etiquette, should be followed.

Make every effort to ensure that the group and full-length photographs look as neat and tidy as possible. They do not have to look stiff, but it is of great importance to avoid scruffiness.

The full-length of the couple is the first main photograph to be taken. Place the couple so that their inside shoulders (i.e. the shoulders nearest each other) are turned away from the camera. This makes the couple stand closer together.

It is essential that the bride's expensive gown looks at its most glamorous. Similarly, the groom's suit must hang correctly and look smart. Pay attention to the groom's jacket. If he is wearing a tie but no waistcoat (vest) make sure his jacket is buttoned. This gives a more tidy appearance. If he does have a waistcoat then the jacket can remain undone. This point should be remembered on all group photographs.

If the jacket pocket has flaps on the outside you must ensure that these are not tucked away inside the pockets. Look at the shirt collar and tidy this up if the points of the collar are jutting up over the jacket. Straighten his necktie. When all this is done (taking only a couple of seconds) the groom is ready for posing.

The groom's left hand can be placed gently on the back of his bride's right elbow. The bride and groom should avoid putting their arms around each other's waists for the formal shots; this makes them look cramped as if they are leaning all over each other and the groom's jacket bunches up on his shoulders.

The bride's hands should be on the floral bouquet, bible or whatever else she may be holding. The groom's right arm should be at his

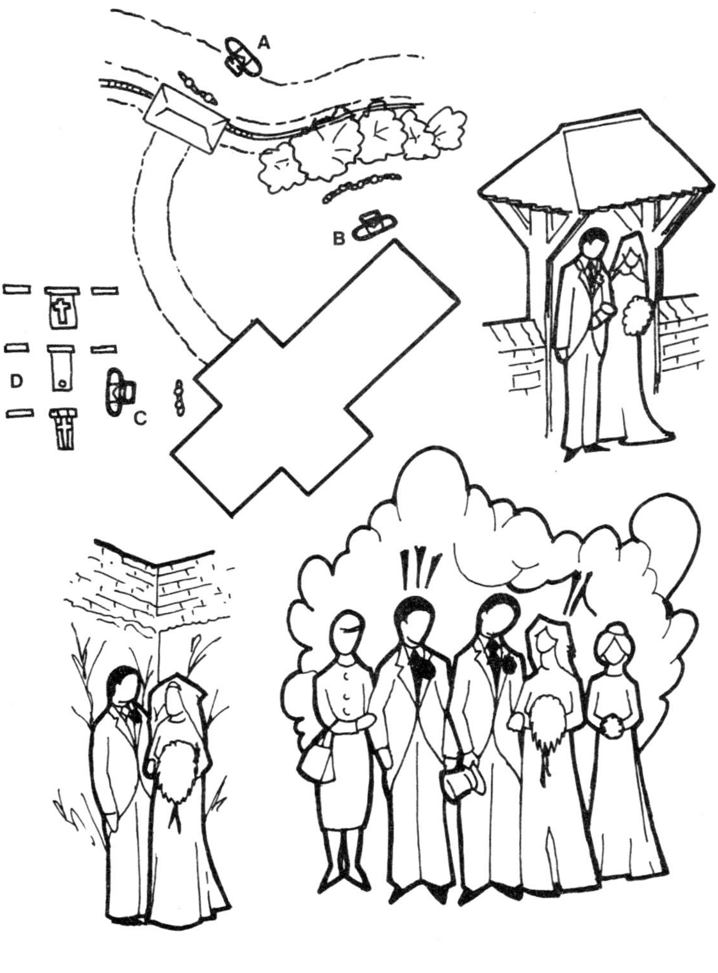

Looking for backgrounds. A. Lychgates can be used to advantage for posing couples under, either in close-up or full-length. B. Trees and foliage make better backdrops than brick walls and should be used whenever possible. C. If you have to use a brick wall as a background then shoot at an angle to the wall. D. Avoid gravestones if you can.

side. *Never* allow the groom to stand with his hands in his pockets or with them clasped in front of him in formal shots. This point also applies to any men appearing in group photographs.

Next, take care of the feet. Viewed from the camera, there should not be any ugly gaps apparent between the subjects' feet.

If the couple are turned at an angle towards each other then the task is much easier. Their feet placed closest to the camera are brought slightly forward. It is also a good technique to show the bride's left toes a little. This confirms that she does have feet and that she has not sunk into the ground! This latter point is of greater significance if she is not very tall.

An upright posture and smiling faces turned towards the camera make for a radiant photograph. The composition looks formal and tidy, but not too rigid.

This basic pose by the couple should be retained for all of the formal groups and it is therefore suggested that for the group photographs the same suitable background is held to enable you to work as quickly as possible. The need to move and reposition your subjects is time-consuming.

Bride and groom – close-up

The hands can be repositioned as you come in close although the couple can hold their basic stance adopted for the previous shot.

If you have arranged the full-length pose sufficiently well then there is little adjustment needed for the close-up.

The couple can be turned just a little bit closer towards each other. The hands can be relaxed so that the groom's left arm *does* go round his bride's waist. Similarly the bride's right arm can be relaxed from the bouquet and that too can be put round her husband's waist. The bride's other hand holding the flowers can then be lifted higher so that it is resting close to the groom's right shoulder and the pose is completed by the couple bringing their cheeks together. The happy faces are turned towards the camera. This is one shot which is frequently used in the local newspapers with the marriage report. As an alternative, swing the couple even further towards each other so that they are face to face, perhaps with their noses touching.

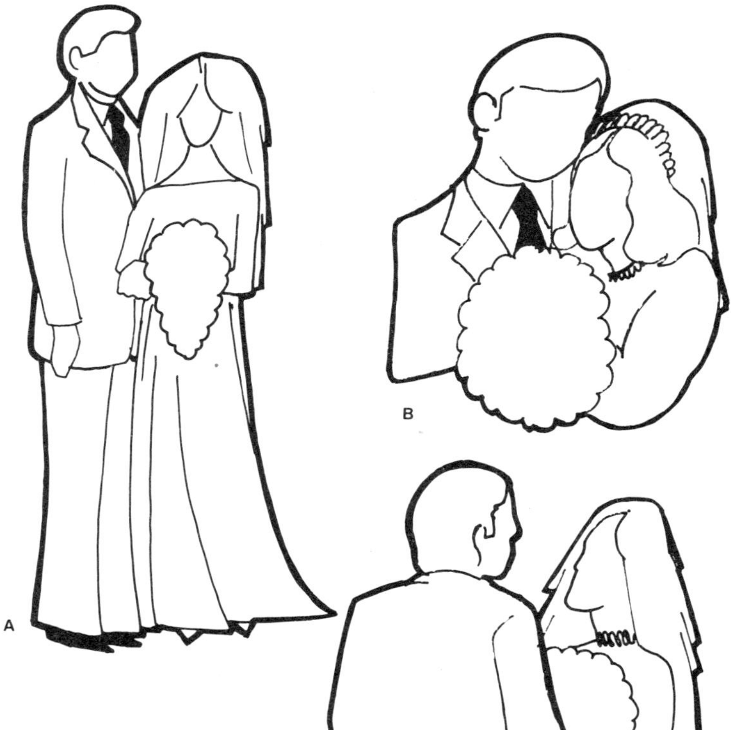

The couple. A. For a full-length study the couple should be turned towards each other so that they look close. Avoid any gaps between legs. B. Close-ups should show the couple with their heads close together in a harmonious study. Keep the camera at the same level as your subjects. C. As an alternative, arrange the groom with his back to the camera and the bride looking at him. Place the couple about one metre (3 ft) apart to avoid the bride looking 'cross-eyed'.

Care must be taken so that the closeness of the bride does not force the groom's jacket to 'buckle' up around his shoulders.
Variations of the close-up study are discussed in the informal section of this chapter.

Bridal group

Feelings of photographers vary as to what, or rather who, constitutes the bridal group. There are no really firm rulings on this subject but basically the group should comprise those that have played a major part in the ceremony. Thus, the bride's father gives her hand in marriage, the best man accompanies the groom during his last moment as a bachelor and the bridesmaids (and page boys of course) attend to the bride. Therefore it is these people which comprise the group.
The groom's parents and the bride's mother sit on the sidelines, as it were, during the actual marriage ceremony and therefore are not officially included in the first group.
The way that the group is set up also depends on the point of view of the photographer. Some think that the bride's attendants should all be on her side of the group along with her father. This leaves only the best man standing by the groom.
Although this may be the correct way of taking the group according to the strictest forms of wedding etiquette, as a photographic composition the group does look very unbalanced. This can be remedied by the best man standing next to the groom, the bride's father (or, whoever else gave her away in the absence of a father) standing next to the bride and the bridesmaids and page boys being spaced evenly on either side. If there are ushers or groomsmen present they can be added.
As with the bride and groom in full-length, everyone should be turned at a slight angle towards the centre of the group. Those on the groom's side turn towards him, those adjacent to the bride turn towards her. Look out for hands clasped crudely in front, open jackets and ties flapping in the wind. Also check that all feet are visible and not hidden under long dresses.
If morning suits are being worn it is normal for the men to hold their top hats in the hand nearest to the camera.

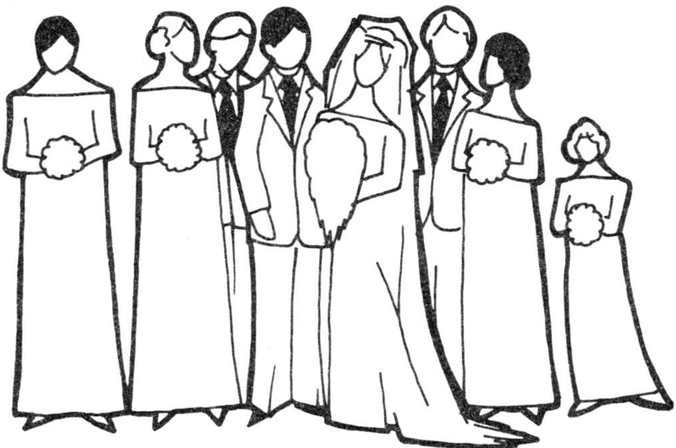

A

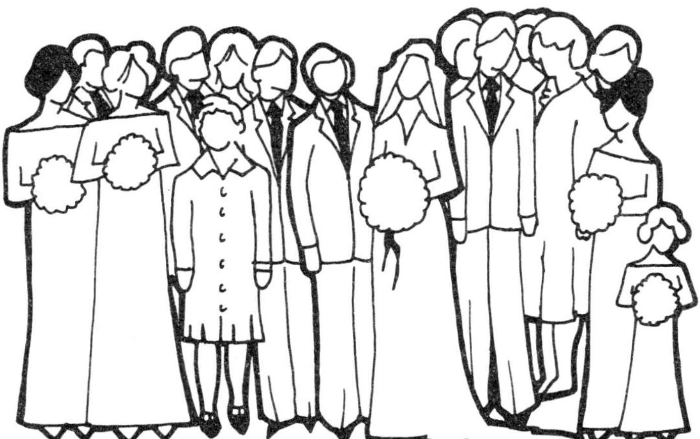

B

Groups. A. Arrange the bridal group as shown and avoid gaps between legs, unbuttoned jackets, cigarettes burning etc. B. On larger groups place people behind front line so that heads can be seen between those in the front line.

Bride and groom – with parents

Many photographers include three groups of this. The first is with all four parents and the next two act as a prelude to the family groups by first taking the couple with the bride's parents, followed by the second taken with the groom's parents.

Once more there is much discussion about the correct way to arrange the parents. Some photographers place the bride's parents next to the groom and vice versa. Most opt, however, for placing the bride's parents next to her and the groom's next to him.

The same basic posing is established but with small groups such as this when there is no more than a handful of people, a three-quarter rather than full-length photograph may make a pleasant change.

Apart from watching for unbuttoned jackets and placing of hands also make sure that ladies' handbags are held in the hand nearest the camera.

Bride and groom – with close families

Having taken the two smaller parent groups described above, you now include any brothers, sisters and their families.

The first close family group consists of the couple flanked by (firstly) the bride's two parents. The father stands next to the bride and the mother is moved across to stand next to her new son-in-law. Then bring in any brothers and sisters of the bride together with their partners (husbands, wives, boyfriends, etc.) and children. Grandparents of the bride can also be added if required and you can round off the groups by adding the bridesmaids to each end to give a little extra colour.

When the bride's close family has been photographed you can keep the group unaltered and go on to the next family group (bride and groom with relations).

When that has been done repeat the process with the groom's close family building towards the large family group.

Bride and groom – with relations

Having taken the immediate family group of the bride you then add the remainder of family. This includes aunts, uncles, first and second cousins and anyone else remotely related. If there is an exceptional number of people you may need to take two or more groups. However, in the UK weddings are seldom this large and one group of each family is all that is normally necessary.

The members of each group should be turned inwards at a slight angle towards the couple. Take care that no gaps appear between the legs and that the subjects are tidy. Ensure that anyone smoking, extinguishes their cigarettes; smoking is an eyesore in any group.

You should avoid shooting the groups against a plain sky because backlighting of this nature can be difficult to correct at printing. Therefore try to use a backdrop of some description. If you have no alternative, the wall of the church if used at an angle behind the arrangement may be all right. A background of trees and bushes is of course ideal but you will seldom meet ideal conditions.

It is usual to place the ladies at the front of the group line-up with the gentlemen at the back so that their faces can be seen in between the heads of those people standing in the front row. Children can be placed at the very front and any taller youngsters can squat on their haunches.

Some photographers carry a set of folding chairs with them when they attend a wedding. This is an excellent idea and enables a larger group to be built up in which everyone can be seen.

Bride and groom – with friends

This group is taken exactly as for the others but this time everyone who has not already appeared in a family group is included. You should be left with the friends of the bride and groom.

If there is an excessive number, you can separate them into the friends of the bride and those of the groom and arrange two groups accordingly.

It is best to aim for an aperture of *f*8 or *f*11 on group photographs to give good depth of field. However, during the winter months low daylight levels often make this difficult.

Opt for flash fill-in if annoying shadows play on the faces of some of the people in the group. Although it is obviously best to try to set your group in a place where there are no heavy shadows this is not always possible and to some extent you must add some extra light with your electronic flash. Avoid posing people into the sun because they will have to squint.

Be careful not to hold your flashgun too close to the camera lens otherwise those terrible red eyes that are commonly associated with flash photographs taken with small compact cameras appear. Similarly do not hold it too far away from the camera as this gives you unsightly shadows that could fall on the faces of those appearing behind the front row of the group.

If conditions prevent you from arranging large groups then take smaller groups which include only the main people. Ask the couple who they really want to include and photograph them accordingly.

Bridegroom with his parents

If you have not managed to take a shot of the groom with his parents before the ceremony try not to forget to do it after. A simple straightforward group taken full- or three-quarter length is appropriate, or you might prefer a more casual shot.

One casual approach is to frame your shot tightly and arrange the mother so that she is pinning the groom's buttonhole flower to his lapel. The father can be behind his wife with his hands placed on her shoulders or as an alternative can be positioned between mother and son but placed slightly in the background. The arrangement takes care of the problem of what to do with the subject's hands.

Bride and groom – with grandparents

You may be requested to take a small group photograph of the couple with their respective grandparents. They are included in the main group depicting the close family but a second more informal group does not go amiss.

If chairs are available then it is a thoughtful gesture to seat the elderly and arrange the couple behind them or similarly seated next to them. This may be easier to stage at the reception.

Another way is to do a three-quarter view and pose the grandmothers looking at the bride's ring.

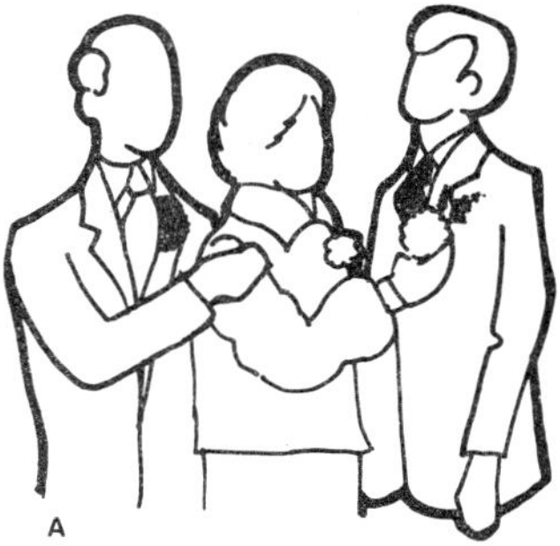

A

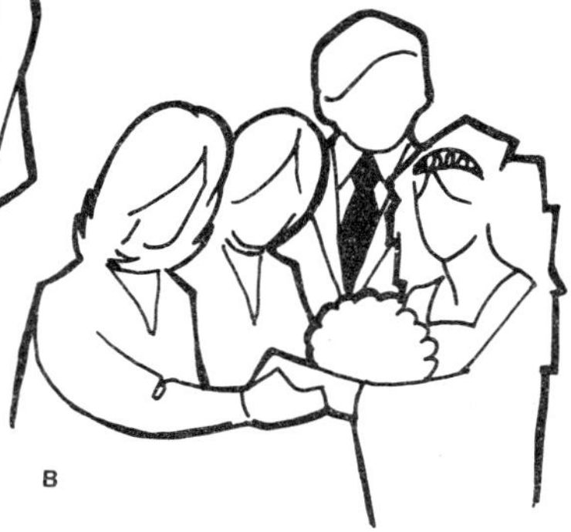

B

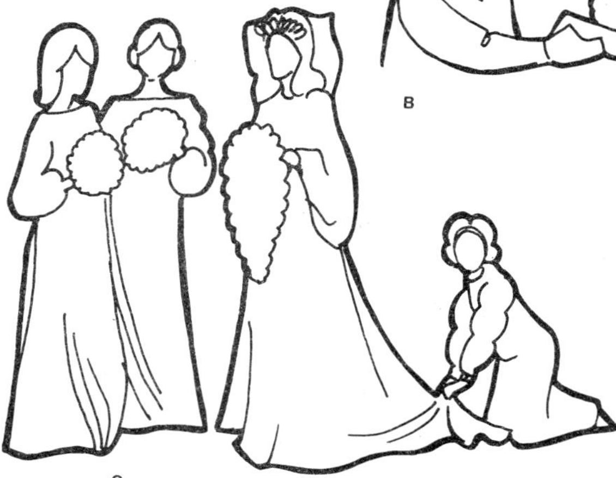

C

Small groups. A. For the photograph of the groom with his parents, pose mother putting on the groom's buttonhole with his father standing at the side with both hands on the mother's shoulder. This pose avoids the problem of where to put hands. B. For the group of both mothers and the couple, arrange for the two mothers to hold the bride's left hand and look at the wedding ring. Groom stands slightly behind the group in the centre. C. When photographing the bride and her attendants, carefully pose the attendants about her and take special care to display the dress, perhaps with one bridesmaid laying out the train.

To arrange this shot the grandmothers are placed to one side of the bride. The groom stands between the senior ladies and his bride so that he is slightly behind them. The grandmothers take the bride's ring hand and hold it in their hands. The expressions should show delight and happiness and their faces can either be turned towards the camera or towards the bride's ring.

The couple's departure

Once the groups have been completed, just a couple more standards remain that can be included. These happen outside the gates of the church and include the following:

Confetti throwing
Bride and groom with limousine
Bride and groom inside car

There are many variations to these basic subjects and these too are described in the casual section.

Bride with bridesmaids

If you have done a home session then you probably already have included this shot, but always try to do another full-length shot of the bride alone and with her attendants after the ceremony. This arrangement is also described as a variation in the casual section.

Confetti throwing

The photographer should attempt to keep the guests from showering the couple with confetti too early in the proceedings, requesting them to wait until the main photographs have been completed. The couple are then taken out of the church onto the pavement where the shot is staged. It is important to take this picture away from the hired cars because chauffeurs, with good reason, object to confetti littering their cars.

Arrange the confetti throwers around the back of the couple and ensure that those forming the barrage are armed with a sufficient handful of the coloured paper. Explain that you will be counting to three and on the third call they are to throw their confetti up *above* the couple. By throwing it above rather than at the bride and groom, a shower effect occurs which can be captured on film. A low angle can be good for recording the couples' expressions as they try to duck the paper rainfall.

It is important to judge the precise moment for pressing the shutter. A second too soon and the faces of the couple are hidden completely by the shower. A fraction too late and the confetti has already landed.

If the shot is successful, the end result can be colourful, amusing and a pleasant addition to any album.

Bride and groom – with limousine

If the couple have rented a limousine to transport them to the reception then this should be included.

A full-length view of the couple beside the car is normal and it is unnecessary to include the whole length of the car unless it is something special such as a Rolls Royce, veteran or vintage car. Horse-drawn carriages likewise fit this special category.

Photographers once again have their own views on the way a car shot should be achieved. It is up to the individual but you can either have the door open or shut. One pose is to shoot the bride inside with one hand on the closed car door, and the groom just behind her. If the car is a Rolls Royce or something similar than move back to include the sleek lines of the bodywork.

Another way is to have the car door open with the bride just about to climb in. The groom can then be positioned so that he is giving her a helping hand into the car.

Unless the daylight is well balanced you may find that the shot needs a little flash fill-in to lift any shadow areas.

Some photographers place the bride on one side of the car bonnet and the groom on the other so that they can hold hands across the hood. If this is pictured from the front with the car grill in the foreground it can make an interesting variation to the norm.

Bride and groom – inside car

It is important to keep the bride and groom on the correct side when taking the car interior shot. The groom should climb into the car first and sit at an angle so that he faces towards the camera. Depending on the make of car, the photographer can either position himself on the front seat or in the doorway of the vehicle. The bride is then placed so that she sits into the groom's shoulder. The couple's cheeks can touch and the groom's arm can be around the bride's waist so that his hand is out of sight.

Avoid the type of arrangement that makes the couple look slumped into the seat. They should appear comfortable but upright.

Try to use available daylight unless it appears too contrasty or restrictive, forcing you to use a shutter speed that is too slow. The soft light which filters into the rear compartment of the car can be very attractive. If flash is used then attempt to soften the effect by bouncing it off the lining of the car ceiling.

Remember to thank the chauffeur for his assistance. It does help to establish a good relationship for future encounters. It is appreciated if you make a point of moving the couple away from the car when the confetti is thrown and then brush them down so that surplus confetti is less likely to end up on the car carpets. Always try to create a good working relationship with chauffeurs and caterers because you never know when you may need to call on them for a favour.

Bad weather

What happens if it rains? Sometimes there really is no alternative but to take your photographs at the reception. If this happens then it is essential to be familiar with the way your flash equipment reacts at various distances. Most guns have a scale on the back that gives the aperture required for shooting at a set range of distances. With computerized guns it is usually satisfactory to let the sensor work out the amount of light emitted for you on short distances. On longer areas of coverage the computerization may be unreliable and the gun will have to be used on full (manual) power and the aperture worked out accordingly.

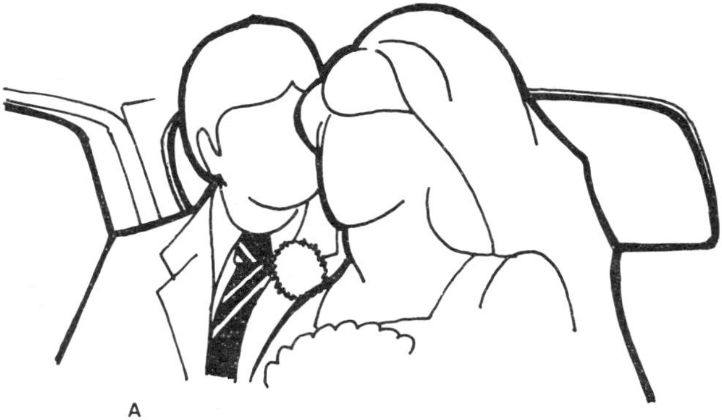

A

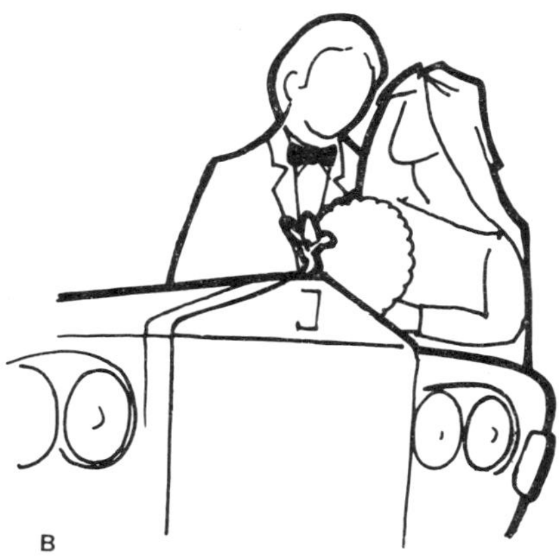

B

The couple with the limousine. A. When the couple are inside the car, then pose them with their heads together and photograph from the bride's side. B. If the limousine is attractive try to incorporate it in your composition. For example, you might focus on the car motif and pose the couple embracing at the side of the car. A medium aperture such as f8 reproduces the bride and groom as slightly out of focus.

The Reception

At most church or registry weddings, the cutting of the cake and the toasts are the only traditional themes that really must be covered at the reception. Additional photographs may be taken at the request of the couple or you may have some imaginative ideas. When a receiving line has been included you may find that you are requested to take a selection of photographs of the couple greeting their guests.

The receiving line

It is less common nowadays for couples to have a receiving line than it was a few years ago, perhaps because this formal greeting of guests tends to become drawn out taking up valuable time at the reception.

The bride and groom line up along with the key members of the bridal party. As the guests enter the reception lounge, they may either be announced by a toastmaster, or they introduce themselves. The toastmaster should be included when present and it can be a good idea to take him aside with the bride and groom for a full-length study.

If you are required to take pictures of guests as they arrive at the reception, it is most important that you obtain a list of those who are to be included. There is little point in taking photographs of every guest when there is a strong chance that they will never sell. You also need the assistance of someone who knows the guests to point out the appropriate people to you. Aim to cover the guests as they are greeted by the couple but shoot so that you capture faces and not back views. It may be necessary to ask the subjects to turn towards the camera as you take your shots but this request may meet with the disapproval of the parents who are keen to welcome the guests as quickly as possible. Try to find a suitable angled viewpoint firstly, in order to minimize the need to halt the line. A high angle may be suitable and you may find that by standing on a chair you gain sufficient height.

Unless the reception is staged outside, you will probably need to work with flash throughout so that you can operate quickly and efficiently.

Cutting the cake

In the majority of cases it is best to pose the couple cutting the cake as soon as the bride and groom arrive at the reception. This enables you to take your leave so that the guests and families can enjoy the reception without you interrupting the occasion further.

There are exceptions of course and some couples may require you to take casual photographs throughout the duration of the festivities.

You may be required to shoot a photograph of the cake on its own. If this is asked for, then comply otherwise do not bother unless the cake is especially grand.

Take the couple to the cake. The groom should again be placed on the correct side of his bride. The placing of the newly-weds should be such that the bride's gown is not hidden behind the cake. The white of the icing sugar and the material of the gown will clash if white is placed behind white. Therefore the bride should stand just a little to one side of the cake with the groom behind it although not hidden from view.

The knife for cutting the cake is first placed in the bride's right hand. The groom's left arm goes round his bride's waist and his right hand now goes on top of the bride's hand which holds the knife. The bride's left hand now goes on top so that three hands are supporting the knife and the ring finger of the bride is visible on top.

The knife blade is then rested on the bottom layer of the cake. The shot is only posed so there is no need for the couple to actually make a cut at this stage; that will follow later on after you have left. The bride can be looking at the groom, they can be looking at each other, downwards in the direction of the cake, or they can look

towards the camera. There are various possibilities but do try to capture happy expressions.
Always attempt to make use of available light on the cake-cutting shot when this is practical. It may mean that the couple must stay motionless while a long exposure is used but the end result is generally worth the effort. If the light is too low then obviously flash. The cake is often placed in front of a window and if possible you should draw the drapes. It is awkward taking the cake and the bridal gown against a bright background but sometimes there is simply no choice. In such cases you may find flash is more acceptable but you must beware of the flash reflecting off glass or other shiny surfaces. The cake can also be tucked away in a tiny corner of a room where there is no space for the couple to be placed behind it. In such circumstances you may be called upon to use all of your ingenuity to make the most of a difficult situation. Be sure to place the bride on the side nearest the camera, with the groom behind.

Toasting

A photograph of the couple toasting one another's health and happiness is the finale of most weddings as far as you are concerned. A close-up of the couple makes a very attractive composition. Again the groom should be standing on the correct side of the bride.
The couple can be arranged with their arms around each others' waists and their cheeks almost touching. Glasses filled with champagne or some other suitable drink should be held by the stems so that the liquid is clearly visible. The glasses should be raised in the toasting position and the lips of the glasses should be touching. Once more, available daylight, or the light from a candelabra perhaps with the use of a starburst filter greatly enhances the study. Unless you have been asked to cover the speeches then your task is over and you have completed your first wedding, and what a tiring experience it turns out to be!

The speeches

If you have been asked to include photographs of the speakers as is likely if the wedding is Jewish, you need to remain at the reception until after the meal.

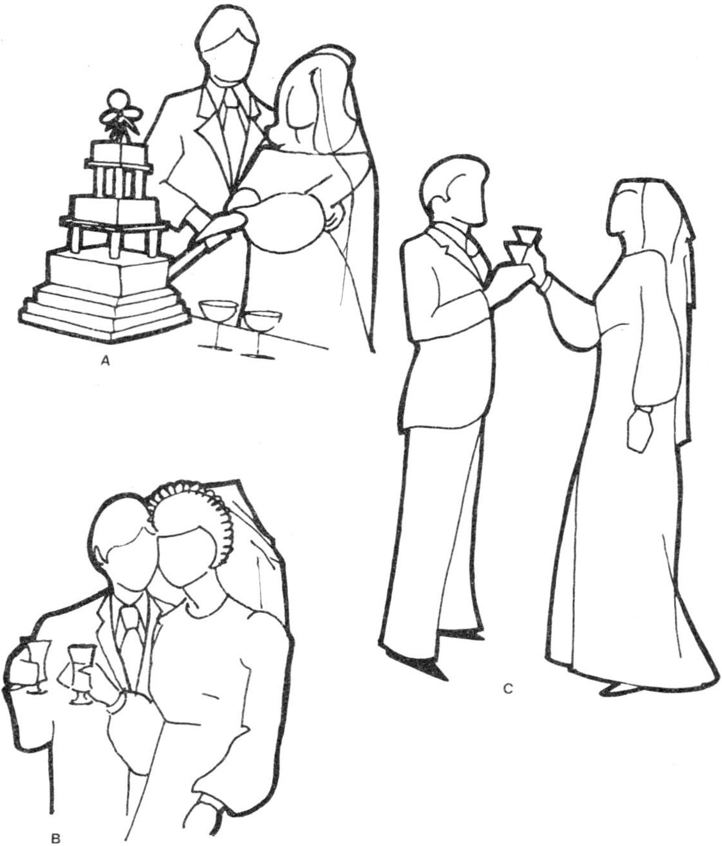

Cutting the cake and toasting. A. Pose the cake-cutting with the bride to the left of the cake so that her dress does not clash with the cake. The groom should be behind the cake. B. If you photograph the toasting in close-up then bring the couple's heads together. Avoid entwining the arms. C. Alternatively, you can photograph the couple toasting as a full-length shot.

Flash is almost certainly essential because speakers are pretty mobile as a rule.
You need to be suitably positioned in front of the speakers who are normally seated on the top table.
Wait for an appropriate expression which reveals something of the speaker's character. If you can stand back far enough to include the bride and groom and their reactions in any shot then so much the better.
You will probably find that the main speeches are given by the bride's father, the groom and the best man. Sometimes uncles or a close friend of the couple may also add a few words and you should be prepared for this.
The speeches are often followed by the presentation of gifts to the bride's attendants and floral bouquets to the mothers of the couple. Try to find a good position to record the groom or best man giving the gifts to the parents. Again, be sure to shoot faces and to frame tightly. Once the speeches have been concluded and the tokens presented there is little else to do other than record the final departure of the couple.

Final departures

In the UK it is not all that common for the photographer to be required right up until the end of the wedding reception; but it is just as well to be prepared for the eventuality should you be asked to stay on.
Commonly the bride leaves the reception at some stage during the informal part of the evening to change into her going-away outfit. This is the signal that the couple are about to leave for their honeymoon, but she will return to say her farewells to the guests.
By tradition the bride tosses her bouquet to her well-wishers at the time she leaves the reception. The folklore behind this act is that the young girl who catches the bouquet will be the next to marry. However, not all brides remember to do this and you may find that you are not called upon.
It is a good idea to record a couple of shots of the couple in the doorway of the reception hall saying their final farewells to the guests.

Then you need to go outside to take one of the couple getting into their car. It is also traditional that the car is decorated by guests with all sorts of slogans painted on the vehicle in shaving cream, lipstick and other materials. Old shoes, tin cans and articles of clothing are also tied to the back of the car. Try to include as much of this as you can as the car pulls away. It may be worthwhile to take a preview shot of the car as the guests are putting the bits and pieces on.

Other Wedding Ceremonies

The information discussed in the preceding chapters is based on the Western Christian marriage, whether Anglican, Roman Catholic or any other denomination.

Other religious practices demand further understanding. Often, they can only really be closely understood from practice or membership of the particular sect or group.

The practices in Eastern religions vary from place to place, even within sects of the same faith. This makes even a general outline outside the scope of a book such as this.

Of course, the general principles of organizing people, composing and lighting your pictures apply to all weddings. However, if you are booked to cover a wedding of a faith you do not know, you should take advice.

Talk to the families involved, and if you can, go along to witness a few ceremonies.

Jewish and Greek Orthodox weddings are often covered by the normal general photographer and therefore the following sections briefly describe weddings held under these faiths.

Jewish weddings

From sundown on Friday to sundown on Saturday is the Jewish Sabbath, therefore Sunday is the main day for Jewish marriages.

There are three main forms of Judaism – Orthodox, Reform and Conservative. Each has its own practices within the main Jewish religion and therefore its own methods of conducting the marriage ceremony.

There is another group within the Jewish faith that the photographer may come across, the Hassidims. These people are basically Orthodox and refuse to violate the Second Commandment 'thou

shalt not make any graven images', and thus, they will not consent to being photographed.
Be careful to respect the wishes of any guest at a Jewish wedding who refuses your request to be photographed. The chances are, that he is a member of this very strict sect.
In Europe, weddings are generally held in the synagogue or temple, but in the USA some ceremonies (with the exception of Orthodox ceremonies) may be held in the home.
It is usual to wear a head covering (cupel or yarmulke) once across the synagogue threshold although the Reform congregations have adopted a rule which either makes the head covering optional or in some cases has banned it altogether.

The Jewish wedding ceremony

The wedding ceremony is very different to that of any other religion. It is staged under a raised canopy known as the Chupa (pronounced 'Hoopah'). This symbolizes the heavens and in most synagogues is a fixture. However photographers may find on occasions at weddings held in the home that a group of men support the Chupa on poles for the duration of the ceremony. Those chosen to perform the role of pole bearer are considered honoured and the task often falls upon uncles of the bride.
The bride is not necessarily escorted by her father as in the Church of England style of wedding. She may be accompanied by both parents, her own and the groom's mother, a brother, uncle or even a close friend. The groom similarly has his escorts. The entrance of the bride is known as the processional but she does not meet the groom at the Chupa but at a predetermined spot on the aisle. The groom then escorts her to the Chupa where the marriage ceremony is conducted by the rabbi. It is common for the bride to kiss her escort and then continue on the arm of the groom to the Chupa. This moment is frequently very emotional and the photographer should ensure coverage if the rabbi has agreed to photography at this stage of the service.
Once under the Chupa, the couple are flanked on either side by the attendants. They can be the parents, bridesmaids, best man and

others close to the couple. The rabbi and cantor (when one is present) stand in front of the couple. The service may be conducted in English, Hebrew or part Hebrew, part English.
The bride and groom each sip from a wine goblet before placing the rings. In the Conservative and Reform denominations there may be two rings, but the Orthodox belief is that only the groom gives a ring to his bride. This follows the bible laws and signifies the groom giving something of material value to his wife in return for her services as a wife. The ring also symbolizes the groom's acceptance of his responsibility as provider for the household.
The photographer must remember that the groom does not place the ring on the third finger of the left hand but on the index finger of the hand. The ring is later moved to the 'traditional' ring finger.
At one stage in the ceremony the rabbi extends a folded or rolled handkerchief to the bride. Holding the other end himself, short vertical motions are made. This signifies the acceptance of the marriage 'contract'. The motion is repeated for the groom.
It is also customary for a glass or bulb to be broken during the ceremony. This symbolizes the destruction of the Hebrew temple in Biblical times.
To avoid the glass from flying in all directions it is normal for it to be wrapped in a cloth. The groom raises his foot, then brings it down and shatters the glass. The couple then kiss, turn around and come down the steps from the Chupa on their way to the signing of the register which is usually conducted in a small room.

Photography during the ceremony

The rules for photography vary depending on the type of Jewish congregation and of course on the rabbi. If the various important photographs cannot be staged during the ceremony it is quite often possible for them to be staged immediately afterwards. This should be checked out with the couple or with the rabbi.
The main photographs that should be included are:

The processional
The 'exchange' – the point where the bride leaves her escorts to take the arm of the groom

The couple on the Chupa faced by the rabbi
The taking of the wine
The placing of the ring or rings
The breaking of the glass with the groom's foot raised and when it crashes down on the glass.
The couple on the steps of the Chupa

Obviously as with any wedding ceremony, this calls for a certain amount of anticipation.
It is important to work with available light during the time the couple are on the dais beneath the Chupa – that is if the rabbi has consented to photographs being taken during the 'live' ceremony. Flash may be used at the time of the processional and when the couple leave the dais. Flash can also be used if the key photographs are staged later once the ceremony has been completed.
There is no real need to go into lengthy explanations about the taking of each shot because they are all basically similar to handle as any photograph taken in church.
It is also worth remembering that in a synagogue it is normal for the men to sit on the left-hand side of the building (viewed from the door) and the women on the right. The congregation is also expected to be silent during the ceremony.
In the UK photographers may also come across the 'Progressive' synagogue. This is another form of Judaism with very liberal attitudes and congregations are more relaxed. It may be possible for photographs to be taken during such wedding ceremonies but once again the rabbi has the last word.

Jewish receptions

Unlike church weddings where the majority of work is done immediately following the ceremony, at Jewish weddings greater importance is placed on the reception.
A few photographs of the couple may be taken outside the synagogue but the majority are taken during the course of the festivities. Receptions are often large and are held in hotels or banqueting suites specializing in Kosher cuisine. In the USA it is more common for receptions to be held in private homes than in the UK.

You will find that you are rushed off your feet during the course of the evening and it is quite normal to take well over 100 photographs depicting various stages of the reception.

This may start with the couple welcoming their guests or, where a guest register is in use, photographs of the various guests signing the book. However, be warned, although you may be presented with a lengthy list of photographs to be included in the coverage quite frequently a large number of your exposures are never bought. It is therefore wise to come to some arrangement with the couple so that you are adequately paid for your work.

Table shots are frequently ordered at the time of booking but once again not always sold. Special emphasis must be given to the top table where the bride, groom, close family, rabbi and special guests sit.

Traditional dancing also plays a key part in the reception and this can be extremely colourful and exciting. However the dances are performed at great speed and you run the risk of being trodden under foot. It is difficult to take photographs during the dancing sessions and therefore it is sometimes best to try to stage a few shots later.

At one stage in the proceedings the bride and groom may be hoisted aloft on chairs and carried around during a dance routine, often to the traditional tune, Hava Nagila. Sometimes the bride and groom will be holding a cloth between them, the purpose of the dance is to try and separate the couple so that they lose hold of the cloth. This is generally performed in a circle and therefore you should either try to get on the inside of the circle or obtain a high viewpoint from outside.

It is also important to pose photographs of the bride dancing with her mother, father and any other special guest. This is because it is very difficult to take decent photographs of couples actually dancing. The posed shot allows you to turn the subjects so that their faces can be clearly seen.

Prior to the start of the wedding dinner the rabbi blesses the proceedings, cuts the bread and blesses the wine. If permitted, you should photograph this part of the reception.

Similarly it is also important to photograph every speaker although this may sometimes take an hour.

The cake cutting and toasting of the couple are just as important as with any other type of wedding, but the shots are seldom posed early on as they would be with a Christian wedding. Instead you photograph the cutting of the cake when it is actually happening. Finally, the couple may request that you stay right until the very end to cover a last few photographs as they depart from the celebrations.

Early on, as soon as you have the opportunity, you should try to bring together the important male and female guests for the guest shots. It is difficult to persuade people away from the festivities to take part in group photographs. If, however, you forget or do not bother with these groups the couple may well be annoyed. It is your responsibility to comply with the wishes of the bride and bridegroom no matter what difficulties may arise and you would be well advised to enlist the best man and the toastmaster to help you get people together. Because these photographs are generally taken during the evening, a corner of the reception suite should be used and flash is, of course, essential.

Jewish weddings are unique when it comes to the role of the photographer. At a church wedding you may expect to put in a few hours with your camera then slip away to have your films processed. The Jewish wedding is a great deal more demanding and normally requires your attendance for the best part of the day *and* the evening. Some couples are reluctant to pay enough to justify the amount of work the photographer puts in; many professional photographers shy away from booking these weddings on the grounds that there is not always sufficient return to make it a worthwhile venture. However, if you can construct a price system that justifies the length of time spent at the wedding and covers the cost of exposing a large number of films then undertaking such lavish occasions may prove worthwhile.

Some photographers may be put off Jewish weddings because they are not of the faith. In practice I have found this makes very little difference.

Greek Orthodox weddings

Greek and Cypriot weddings are colourful occasions which again have a flavour all of their own. The first wedding of this kind you are sent to cover is usually quite a traumatic experience because there is always so much going on around you it is quite easy for you to be swept aside in the festivities.

Greek weddings are generally held in churches or cathedrals of the Orthodox faith. The ceremony conducted in church is very unusual. There is no objection at all to photography. Indeed, if you are hired as official photographer you will find that you will have to struggle against guests with ciné cameras, lights and even instant-picture cameras, each competing for the best viewpoint at the altar. The whole ceremony is conducted amidst a crowd of guests and well-wishers.

It is normal for both the bride and the bridegroom to have their respective best men and women. These are normally close friends or key members of the families and they pay the couple for the privilege. There is apparently no limit to the number of best men and women and it is therefore quite normal to have eight or nine on either side of the couple.

The services are always conducted in Greek unless one of the couple is of a different nationality and is unable to speak the language. There is no need to go into great detail about the service because you can cover the whole occasion as you see fit. Greek couples place great importance on the ceremony and therefore any photographs taken during the various stages are likely to be popular. At one point long white ribbons are attached to the heads of the couple and these are signed by others taking part in the ceremony. The rings, once placed on the fingers of the couple are then removed by the best men and women and other guests positioned around the altar and the groom's ring is placed on the bride's finger and vice versa. This ritual is repeated many times.

Photographs are taken after the ceremony in the church grounds or park as at any other western church wedding but the photographer is usually required for longer at the reception. It is important of course to cover the cutting of the cake and the toasts but the dancing is also an important aspect of the reception and should be photographed.

At one stage the bride dances and guests pin money on her gown. This is the time when the best men and women pay for their

privilege and when other guests may offer their gift to the couple. It is quite normal for the bride to look like a walking payroll and you certainly should not fail to capture her decked in banknotes. Sometimes the groom joins his bride in this dance and you should not miss posing a shot of the couple together.
The Greek Orthodox ceremony is not recognized under British law and in order to comply with the constitution it is necessary for the couple to go through a simple civil ceremony at a registry office. This normally takes place a few days before the religious ceremony but you may not be required to attend, greater emphasis being placed on the church ceremony.

The civil ceremony

Today there is a greater tendency for couples to choose a marriage ceremony held in a civil registry office. The civil ceremony in most cases is now conducted in a very personal and pleasant atmosphere and many couples feel the short ten minute proceedings are preferable to the longer ritual of a church service.
Weddings held in registry offices in the UK are now growing in size. It is not uncommon for over 100 to attend. This affects the photographer. A couple of years ago a professional would not have expected to earn a great deal from a civil marriage. Today the situation to some extent has reversed and couples marrying in civil ceremonies are becoming big spenders, possibly because the lower cost of the ceremony leaves them with more to spend on other things.
It is quite common in some countries for couples to go through both a religious ceremony and a civil one. The latter forms the legal part of the marriage contract whilst the former is to satisfy religious beliefs. When this is the normal practice, it is usual to confine the professional photographic coverage to the religious ceremony, although records of the civil proceedings as well are becoming more popular.
When you photograph a wedding, no matter whether it is conducted in a church or registry office, you should give it the same treatment. You should attend the bride's home before the ceremony and,

similarly, take the normal arrival shots. The only part about a civil marriage that is different is the ceremony. The registrar is actually the person who completes the details in the register and he or she usually sits at a table filling out the necessary documents while an assistant goes through the ceremony with the couple.

At some centres the ceremony may be interrupted as the rings are placed to allow photographs to be taken. Enquire about this when you arrive at the registry office. Some registrars prefer to complete the ceremony and then allow the photographer time to stage the ring ceremony and signing of the register.

The photographs of the placing of the ring are usually easier to take than during a church service. There is generally more room to move about and flash can be used if you want to, although, available light can be very appropriate in some registry offices. They are usually more brightly lit than churches.

It is best to take the photograph at an angle from the groom's side so that the face of the bride can be clearly seen.

The groom takes the bride's left hand and simulates the placing of the wedding ring. The couple can either be looking at each other or they can be turned to look towards the camera. The misty attachment can be used with great effect on this shot.

You can then re-seat the couple for the signing of the book. This is conducted in much the same way as it would be in the church except that both the bride and the groom can be seated if preferred. It is not necessary to include the officiating registrars in any of the photographs although no harm is done if you do, providing they are agreeable.

The remainder of the photographs can be taken in the registry office grounds, a local park or other location and the pattern follows the same lines as for church weddings. The only exceptions are that there may not be any bridesmaids, and witnesses replace the duties of the best man and the bride's father.

Special Wedding Problems

The wedding timetable

It goes without saying that you must ensure that you arrive on time for the occasion. Equally, your coverage must not hold up events longer than is necessary and on no account should you make the bride late for her ceremony by overindulgence in your home session. How long should each part of the ceremony take to cover? This is not a straightforward question to answer but to some extent generalizations can be made from examining a typical western style wedding.

There are of course differences between weddings held in the UK compared to the USA. In the UK it is common for the marriage ceremony to be held near the bride's residence. In the USA it is equally common for the bride to reside near where the ceremony will take place but in some cases the distances may be fairly substantial. Also, some churches in the USA provide dressing rooms where the bride or bridegroom may prepare for the ceremony rather than at their own homes. It is therefore up to you to ensure that you are familiar with the location of the bride's home in relation to the place of the ceremony.

You should then prepare a timetable according to the travelling distance. Forty five minutes to an hour should leave ample time for taking a series of portraits at the bride's home.

However, if the bride's family wish a lot of photographs to be taken at the home, you will have to make a decision on how much time you require. The bride should then be advised so that she will allocate sufficient time for all the photographs. It is always a good idea to obtain advance information from the couple about any special photographs that they may want taken.

Allow more time than it *should* take to reach the ceremony from the bride's home. You can never be certain about traffic conditions and

there is always the possibility that you may end up having to change a wheel of your car en-route. Also make a point of finding out if any local events such as carnivals, sporting occasions or holiday traffic are likely to hold up your progress. If you find any problems that are likely to occur, then you should notify the bride about these and turn up at her home a little earlier to allow for these hold-ups.
The minimum of time should be taken outside the church covering the bride's arrival. Certainly no more than five minutes should be spent otherwise you might make the bride late for the ceremony.

The schedule inside the church

Inside the church or registry office you must be prompt and precise about your coverage, working almost by instinct in order that you do not delay the proceedings. You do not need to stop the bridal procession as they come up the church aisle because this shot is taken as they walk towards you. A brief moment is all it should take to arrange the couple in the doorway while you hold up the following procession to take your photograph.

The schedule outside the church

Outside the church, twenty minutes should be enough time for an experienced operator to complete a range of shots including formal groups, close-up studies and casual arrangements. With large wedding groups you may find that you need a little extra time. If you take much longer you will find that the guests may become irritable because they are being kept waiting.
When you are asked to take an excessive number of photographs which the couple require as 'extras' to your normal coverage, then you should inform them that it will take longer to complete your work.

The timetable at the reception

Once at the reception, shortly after the couple arrive, you need to take them aside to arrange the cake-cutting and other photographs.

Ten minutes or so should be all the time it takes unless you are booked to remain at the reception for the duration, in which case you can take your shots as and when the couple may direct.

In the USA it is common, as mentioned in the introduction, for photographers to complete part of their work at a time set aside from the occasion. This therefore leaves the ceremony free to be enjoyed without the photographer holding up the proceedings. This method involves either studio sessions or the use of natural beauty spots as alternative settings for the key members of the wedding party. Such sessions may be staged well in advance of the wedding or even on the morning of the occasion. In the UK this method of coverage is not usual although it will probably be adopted as couples begin to demand more comprehensive coverage of their wedding.

A typical schedule

Shown below is a specimen table for an average Western church wedding. The wedding is set for 3.00 p.m. and the photographer must take a home session, with no special requirements, before the ceremony.

Having ensured all of your equipment is working correctly and that you have not forgotten your film, you set out for the bride's home.

1.50 p.m. Arrive bride's home. Allow 30–45 minutes to take a selection of studies.

2.30 p.m. Photograph bride leaving home and set out before limousine to reach church before the bride.

2.40 p.m. Arrive at church (assuming that the bride lives within a mile of the church and that there are no traffic problems). Photograph the groom, best man and key guests.

3.00 p.m. Bride and father enter church with attendants for the ceremony.

4.00 p.m. Use part of the ceremony time to survey the church grounds for suitable backgrounds (if you could not do this before). Ceremony ends and after signing register couple leave church.

4.25 p.m. You should have completed your coverage and bride and groom have got into their limousine ready for the journey to the reception.

5.00 p.m. Couple arrive at reception.

5.20 p.m. After greeting their guests, you take the couple aside to complete your coverage with cake-cutting, toasting and any other photographs required.

6.00 p.m. After a brief period completing your coverage you should have departed and be on your way home or to the colour laboratory.

Most church ceremonies take only 20–30 minutes and civil weddings take about 10–15 minutes. Timings must, however, be based on the individual circumstances and the above list is therefore only a guide. Some weddings of different denominations may require much longer for your coverage. It is always wise to check the timings and duration of the ceremony before accepting the booking.

Non-Caucasian weddings

If you are asked to cover a variety of unfamiliar ceremonies then you should 'sit in' on a few in order to grow accustomed to the rituals. However, a good many non-Caucasian people follow the same Christian religions as most of your customers. Therefore there should be no fundamental difference in the way you cover the occasions.

The main problem which worries photographers is the stark contrast between the skin tones of the subjects and the bride's dress. Certainly this can be very marked and light readings must be taken with extreme care. If you expose for the bride's gown then the faces of your subjects will be almost unrecognizable. By exposing for the skin tones the dress can then appear grossly overexposed. Exposure is however a problem that you learn to live with. It is difficult to create a happy medium by taking an exposure setting in between the two readings of bride's gown and skin tones because the detail in the subjects' faces may be lost. It is preferable to suffer the loss of detail in the bride's gown in order to keep your subjects' faces well defined.

A skilful printer, even one using an automated machine, should be able to establish a happy colour balance in the end product. An expert colour grader can also be your 'best friend' when the proofs or test prints are balanced for colour. Skin tones are frequently difficult to print correctly, more so when there is a marked contrast between the people in the same composition.

What do you do when you happen to be covering a wedding where the groom is of white skin and the bride is coloured? This situation presents a very tricky exposure problem. You could opt for a reading that is half way between the skin tones of the couple. For example, if your exposure meter reads *f*8 from the face of the groom and *f*4 from the bride's face, an exposure of *f*5.6 should give sufficient exposure to hold the detail in both faces.

Elderly persons

Some of the most enjoyable weddings to cover can be those involving an elderly couple. With senior citizens you are likely to find (if they have been married before) that there will be several generations present. They may each have their own respective children, grandchildren and even great-grandchildren. They must all be carefully grouped with the couple for the photographs.

Exactly how you go about covering an elderly persons' wedding depends much upon the situation at the time. If, for example, the weather is bad then you should not keep them outside, exposed to the elements, even for a couple of photographs although with a younger couple this may be acceptable.

You also need to consider the mobility of the couple. You could find that one or other of them is unable to walk very far or they may not be able to stand for very long. Whatever the situation you should aim to take as little time about your coverage as possible.

A good course of action is to leave the majority of your photographs until the reception where time can be taken to arrange your groups so that the bride and groom can be seated. Seated groups seem to work well with elderly people because it is possible to group the younger members of their families casually around them.

Coverage need not be drastically different from any other wedding, although you may wish to reduce the number of photographs that you take. It may be wise to mention to the couple the type of photographs that you usually take. It is very likely that they will not like the more modern approaches and compositions such as misties and superimposed montages. If you aim for a formal and traditional approach then you cannot go far wrong. In any case it is likely that an elderly bride and groom will show greater appreciation of the simpler approach providing you do not forget to include all the family.

When it comes to presenting the finished prints remember that elderly people may not have as much money to spend on your services as a younger couple.

Double weddings

Occasionally you may be asked to photograph a double wedding. This is a joint ceremony between two couples and usually happens when two sisters, brothers or twins decide to share the occasion. Close friends who have become inseparable over the years, may also adopt a double wedding ceremony. Generally however, double wedding ceremonies are not at all common although more are held in the USA than in the UK.

Services are conducted in much the same way as at any other wedding. When the actual marriage vows are exchanged the priest normally takes each couple in turn and completes the procedure before going on to the second couple. Both couples complete their vows before moving to the vestry where the marriage certificates are signed.

From your viewpoint as the photographer, you must expect a busy afternoon. Exactly how you go about your coverage depends mainly upon the requirements of the couples concerned.

It is important of course to maintain the double theme although the two couples are shown together only in some of the photographs.

Groups, especially when many of the guests are concerned with both couples as they generally are, should include both brides and both grooms on the arms of their respective partners. This also applies for small family groups depicting close members of each party, such as parents, brothers and sisters.

Often the bridesmaids and best man are common for both couples and these can normally be included in one shot. Other formal photographs, such as the traditional full-length of the bride and groom, can be shot separately of each couple and as a foursome.
Apart from the main groups, most of the photographs should be taken as they normally would be, showing only one couple. The couples coming back up the church aisle should be taken separately. So too should the couple posed looking back over their shoulders as they stand in the church doorway. Close-ups, casual misties and other key photographs are taken of each couple separately.
You need to keep your wits about you. If an assistant can be taken along to give you a hand then so much the better. There are countless opportunities when you can take advantage of the 'double' theme and a certain amount of light-heartedness can be included in your picture series. You must work hard and fast because you have to take most of your shots twice which involves re-posing the couples. You should not miss the opportunity to photograph a double wedding if you regard yourself as an enterprising photographer; there is a great deal to be made of such an occasion.

People of awkward proportions

This may sound a strange section to include. However, at some time in your career as a wedding photographer you are bound to come across people who do not, in every way, conform to average shape (weight, height, etc.).
At the vast majority of weddings, emphasis should be placed on the bride and she should receive most of the 'limelight'. When you arrange a shot showing both the bride and the groom you normally shoot slightly from the bride's side rather than from the front. This is because the groom is generally slightly larger than the bride and you do not want him to dominate the photograph. As an example, the shot taken of the couple sitting in the back of the bridal limousine is taken with the groom normally placed in the far corner of the seat with the bride seated nearest to the camera. This allows for the groom's additional height or weight to be minimized so that the bride does not look dwarfed by his presence. This is the rule of

thumb throughout the coverage but on occasions you need to revise this theory.

There are times when you arrive to find that the bride is anything but tiny. When the couple are together, it is the bride who dwarfs the groom. In this case you must reverse the arrangements so that your photographs are taken with the bride placed farthest from the camera and the groom in the foreground.

The situation can be awkward particularly if the bride is a great deal taller than the groom. On close-up studies the bride can incline her head downwards to bring it closer to the groom's head. Although difficult, with care and a strong sense of composition, the situation can be overcome so that the resulting photographs are acceptable.

Some of your shots can be taken using props which allow the bride to sit down, although much care in arranging the gown needs to be taken. There are key shots where the differences of height or weight stand out but this really cannot be entirely avoided. Be certain not to make a point of noting the differences to the couple. Just try to cope with it as best you can without making it too obvious in your compositions.

You may also find on occasions that you are called to photograph the weddings of sick or deformed persons. Again, great care must be used to ensure that your photographs are taken in a natural way. Sometimes one or other of the couple may be a cripple in which case your shots may either have to be arranged with the person seated in a wheelchair or on crutches. In cases such as this you must do your best to present a tidy set of photographs.

People with scars can also present a problem. If the scars are old then it is unlikely that the couple will be self-conscious about them. On the other hand, if the marks are more recent, then there will probably be a natural reluctance to have any close-up photographs taken. If you sense this then you should leave out the close-up studies and concentrate on full-length pictures. If however the scar appears only on one side of a person's face then you may try taking the shot from the other side so that the scar is hidden from view. This applies even when it may become necessary to rearrange the couple so that the groom technically is standing on the 'wrong' side of the bride.

Lastly, you must also ensure that no prominent natural features such as long noses and double chins intrude on the composition. Care when turning the subject's head in close-up studies helps to eliminate sharp and defined noses. A full flat-on shot showing the subject looking down almost certainly highlights the nose and this type of shot is best avoided.

Double chins are also common. Try to shoot from a camera position that is slightly above your subject's neck line. They are then looking either directly towards the camera at eye level, or upwards a little towards it. Never ask your subject to look downwards if the chin is prominently double as this will emphasize the feature.

Sharp, long or pointed chins should also be angled to lessen the effect. If in any doubt, direct your subject's head movements from the viewfinder of the camera until you are satisfied that you have caught their most flattering angle. In most cases practice teaches you the best angles to use for the particular facial problem you come across.

Wedding Photography with a Difference

The previous chapters explain the methods of covering a wedding in the basic form. The photography mentioned deals with coverage in the 'old sense' and examines the standard poses that have been adopted since photography became a part of the wedding occasion. This section is devised to go one step beyond the routine – to discuss a brighter form of coverage – the type the public are now rightly demanding.

This chapter does not go through the whole wedding sequence listing the alternative ways of covering each photograph. It is up to you to work on your own ideas to bring out *your* creative attributes. However, this chapter offers a few examples which will help make your wedding package a little more exciting.

Use of depth of field

One method photographers of weddings rarely employ is the control and use of restricted depth of field. Most wedding photographs are taken with the subjects standing in more or less a straight line. If the bride is photographed with her attendants, they are often placed in a line either side of her. The same goes for groups or any other aspect of the wedding series. There is no real need or reason to place everyone in the same plane. You can make full use of foreground and background for placing the subjects; this results in a more lively form of photography.

You can restrict the depth of field to your advantage. Picture those in the foreground in focus with those in the background only suggested, being out of focus. Alternatively, you can confine sharp focus to those at the back. Or, or course, you can follow traditional practice and shoot the whole photograph in sharp focus. Each picture needs to be thought out on its own. To start you off, here are a few examples of manipulating the depth of field.

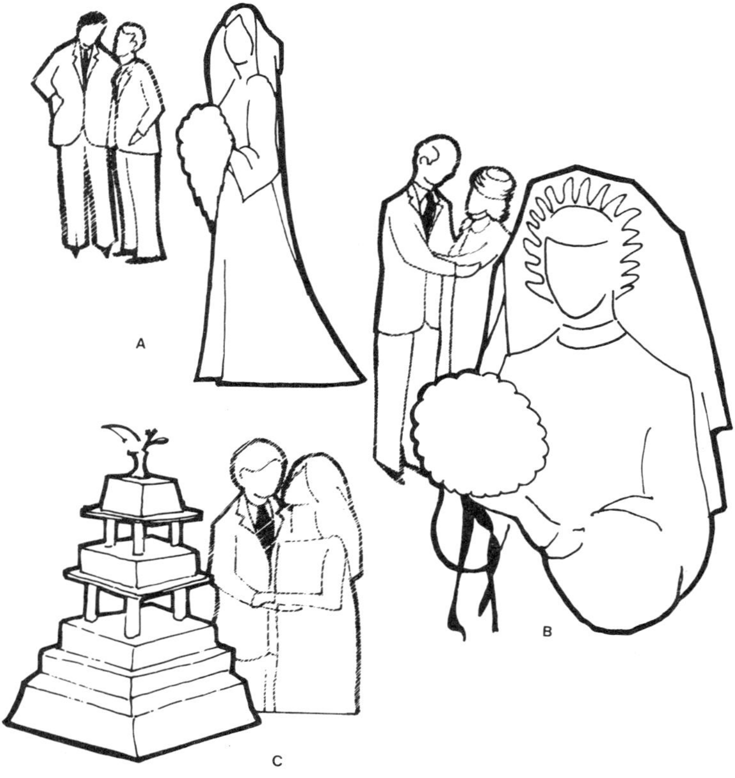

Controlling depth of field for effect. A. The bride can be placed in the foreground with the groom and best man in the background. The bride appears sharply focused and the other two are slightly out of focus. Experiment with different aperture settings to get the desired effect. B. A similar shot can be taken with the bride in the foreground and the bride's parents in the background. C. A further example of this technique is to photograph the cake with the couple in the background. This photograph is more appealing than a shot of the cake on its own.

The bride full-length with groom and best man

Pose the bride normally in full-length fashion but instead of placing the bridegroom and his best man at her side, stand them in the background where they are casually posed leaning against a tree or wall, perhaps with arms folded and in conversation.

Then focus the camera on the bride and choose an aperture to give the desired depth of field required for the subject. A stop of about *f* 8 (on a 6 × 6 cm camera) portrays the pair in the background as recognizable but not too sharp. Of course, the most suitable aperture depends on the distance between the bride, and the groom and the best man. A smaller lens opening makes them sharper and a wider aperture, more out of focus. It is usually best to opt for a slight softness of focus on the groom and best man – the emphasis is thus kept on the bride.

You might try the same method for taking the bride with her parents, although a low light level indoors may make flash essential. The bride is placed in the foreground, perhaps three-quarter length (depending on the space available) and the parents slightly out of focus in the background where once again the pose suggests that the parents are watching over their daughter.

Bride and groom with wedding cake

Another photograph that can be improved by controlling the depth of field is one depicting the couple with their cake. This time, instead of placing the couple in the cutting position, turn them towards each other and ask them to kiss. By choosing a fairly wide lens aperture and sharply focusing on the cake you picture the couple in soft focus; which is much more attractive than featuring them pin sharp. Exactly the same treatment can be applied to an outdoor shot of the couple kissing beside their limousine. If the car is a Rolls Royce then the composition works extremely well. If you sharply focus on the silver lady emblem of the car, the couple will be captured softly out of focus.

However, a word of warning; do not overuse the method otherwise it will cease to be effective.

Relaxed close-up studies

Too often the close-up shots of the bride, groom or guests are taken with their heads turned straight towards the camera without any imagination. Better studies result if the subjects are placed in a casual manner, perhaps leaning across a gate or onto a chair back. Instead of the routine study of the groom with the best man, try the same sort of pose mentioned in the last section. The two men can be leaning against a tree in conversation. Take it in a manner which suggests they have not been aware of the presence of the camera.

The groom on his own looks more light-hearted if he is taken as he leans on the top bar of a gate or fence. He could even have his chin resting in his hands. Whichever way, a casual approach lends more interest and life to an average subject.

Shooting the subjects through the branches of a tree helps add a little sparkle to a close-up study. The addition of the misty attachment also creates mood.

Remember to work with a shallow depth of field, perhaps a stop of *f*4 or *f*5.6, to throw the background behind your subjects well out of focus to give that 'haloed' effect that is especially enhancing on outdoor portraits.

Bride and groom studies – a change in approach

By all means keep the formal pictures of the couple within your series but add your own special studies as well.

Do not be afraid to seat your subjects on a park bench or on the grass if the ground is dry and clean.

If the bride is wearing a garter and wants to show it off then she can recline on a seat with the appropriate leg raised and her garter showing. The groom and best man can be added to the study for better effect, their faces perhaps showing good-humoured surprise.

The couple sitting in peaceful conversation on a lawn, especially if the grass is long and wild, adds a great deal of impact to a romantic study. Look around you, keep your eyes open and watch for possible better studies.

Groups turned informal

The group photographs are less easy to change, particularly if they contain a large number of guests. Smaller groups can be split up so that the bride and groom remain in the centre and the guests are arranged into smaller groups around the couple. This works well when taken in a garden at the reception and the guests are given glasses to raise in a toast to the couple.

Candle-lit photographs

The addition of a candelabra can work wonders in a couple of photographs shot at the reception. Some photographers carry their own candles in the car just in case the caterers fail to provide any. They are not always used, but if the weather is bad and you have to resort to shooting all of your photographs inside then you have an extra ace up your sleeve.

The glow of burning candles does add a certain air of romance to a close-up study of the newly weds. This works particularly well on the toasting shot with the couple placed behind the candles. You may also like to add a serious study of the bride on her own, her face turned towards the candles and her hands clasped prayer-like in front of her.

Candles are really attractive especially when you use their own output of light for the exposure. Many good studies are ruined because the photographer added electronic flash to his exposure. If you intend to use candles then go all the way and shoot using a long exposure with your camera mounted on a tripod. The exposure may be as long as one second but it is frequently less. If the couple are placed with their heads touching in a harmonious pose then they can probably keep still long enough for this relatively long exposure. Take a reading from both shadow and highlight areas of the subjects' faces and opt for an average exposure between the two. If the highlights, for example, give a reading of *f*5.6 and the shadows give *f*2.8, then a camera setting of *f*4 gives the best result.

If you feel the need to use flash, aim for bounced light from a wall or ceiling and use it sparingly as a fill-in light. A red filter over the flash head can produce additional effect and adds a warm glow.

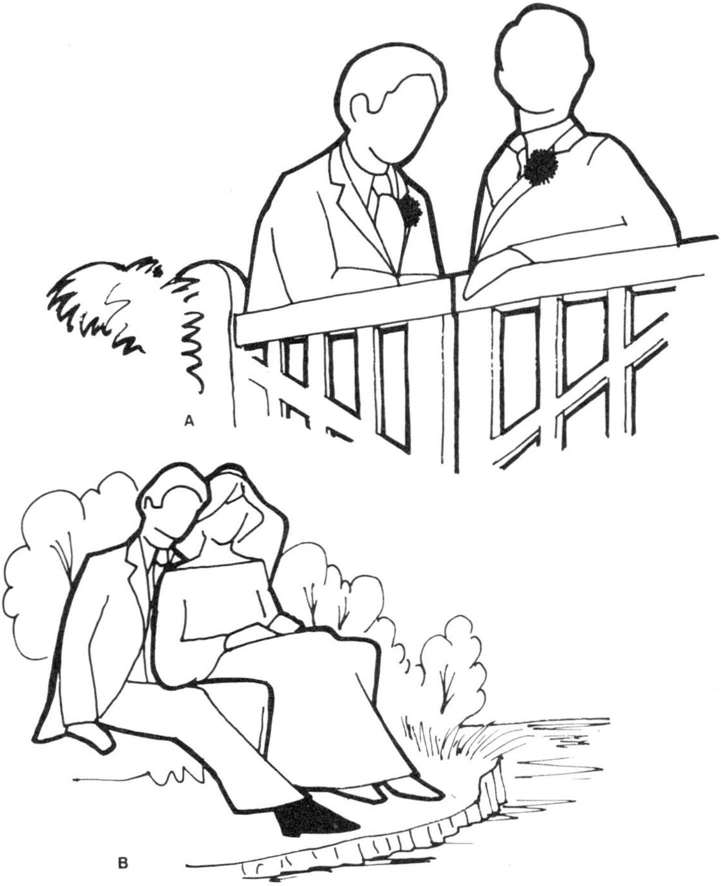

Use of props. A. An alternative to the fairly rigid style of photograph is to let your subject pose in a relaxed manner leaning on a gate. B. Ponds or rivers can make very attractive surroundings for photographs. You could seat the couple on the banks looking at the water.

Other Special Occasions

There are a great many other occasions, religious and otherwise, each special in their own way and requiring the attentions of the photographer. Private and public parties, gatherings, works outings – each a special occasion – worth recording, worth remembering, yet so often neglected photographically.

Professional photographers are seldom hired for such occasions. Money may not be available to pay out in fees. Often the amateur is given the chance. But, even if you have not been hired to do the job, take along a camera because there could be the chance of grabbing a few worthwhile shots and may be some profit into the bargain.

This part of the book examines some of the social occasions that can be covered by professionals and by amateurs with a keen eye. Those mentioned are by no means definitive. Every day of the year, almost every hour, some occasion is taking place, which is worth photographing.

Religious occasions

The main religious occasions other than weddings are such events as christenings, barmitzvahs and confirmations.

Christenings

A christening is the occasion when a child (or for that matter an adult) is baptised into the christian religion. Christenings are often held en masse. Several families may be brought together on a given date to participate in a joint baptism ceremony. There is plenty of scope here for photographers to record the occasion although professionals are hardly ever hired for the event.

The permission of the clergy must again be forthcoming before you can photograph in church. Permission is however more readily given than for weddings and therefore there should be no problem.

In the Church of England, a short ceremony is normally followed by the actual blessing of the child or adult in holy water at the font. Young babies and children are often overawed by the occasion and burst into tears. Be sure to capture the tears as the vicar makes the mark of the cross in water on baby's forehead.

Other photographs that should be included are small groups depicting the parents with their child together with the officiating clergy, the couple holding the infant, the vicar holding the infant with the parents looking on and, of course when possible, the infant alone.

Occasions vary from family to family. Some gatherings may be restricted to include just the parents. Others may involve grandparents, godparents, aunts, uncles and friends. If the occasion is attended by these people then you should include them in the photographs.

A number of group photographs should also be taken outside the church similar to those taken at a wedding.

A party normally follows the baptism ceremony. It is important to take further pictures here, perhaps of the child in a change of clothing and one of the parents drinking a toast to the child.

First Communion

When Roman Catholic children reach the age of six or seven they are considered old enough to take Holy Communion. Usually a day is set aside for a group of children to take their very first Communion.

The children are usually dressed all in white, the girls frequently looking like little brides. At the appropriate time they file up to the altar where they receive Communion from the priest.

Photography is often possible within the church and therefore you should aim to picture the particular child you are interested in as he or she receives Communion.

Confirmations

These occur chiefly when children are sworn publicly into a particular religious faith. Confirmation often takes place when a child is twelve or thirteen and marks the moment when that child has assumed readiness to become a full member of his or her particular religion.
Photography may or may not be permitted during the ceremony and therefore you should first check with the clergy.
Confirmations within the Jewish religion mark the end of a child's teaching at the synagogue where he learns Hebrew and the history of his religion.
As with other religious ceremonies, photographs should be taken of the children involved as portrait studies, with their parents and other prominent guests. The priest or rabbi should also be included in one or two shots.

The Barmitzvah

The barmitzvah is unique to the Jewish faith and takes place when a boy reaches manhood. The ceremony can be set for any time after the boy's thirteenth birthday but never before.
Girls of similar age have their own ceremony, known as the batmitzvah, but this is not regarded with the same importance as the boy's ceremony. The wedding is considered the most important occasion in a girl's life but the barmitzvah is the boy's chief occasion.
Photography is not normally permitted during a barmitzvah ceremony and therefore key shots such as the boy in the pulpit are frequently staged, either before the Sabbath or after the ceremony, depending on the attitude of the rabbi and the type of congregation.
It is important to include the benediction of the wine and the bread afterwards if this is allowed.
The reception is normally held on the Saturday immediately following the synagogue ceremony. Portraits of the boy are called for, together with shots of him with his parents, grandparents and other people closely associated with the family. Table shots may also be requested but it is best to check with the host prior to

shooting because some families become upset if unrequested photographs are included in the coverage.
Dancing photographs should also be taken showing the boy with his mother, grandmother, sister, aunt, etc. You are advised to pose these photographs so that their faces are visible.
The highlight of a reception is often the candlelighting ceremony. The boy is called to blow out fourteen candles that have been placed by close members of the family and friends on a cake.
There may be certain variations at some receptions. The boy may be called to a 'tree of life' where fourteen flowers have been placed or, instead, there maybe a jigsaw puzzle containing fourteen pieces. This, when completed, shows a photograph of the barmitzvah boy. You ought to picture the boy with whatever is proferred for this part of the ceremony.
The guests then usually sing 'Happy Barmitzvah Boy' and 'Happy Birthday' to the boy. Speeches may follow and should take care to include each of the speakers in your coverage.

Engagement parties

Many couples now marry without having a term of formal engagement. However engagement parties are still held in numerous cases. Engagement parties are sometimes held in halls but more often simple house parties are thrown in a private house.
You should make a point of taking individual portraits of each of the couple, perhaps with one or two misties for good measure; then again as a pair also using the misty. You can then take a few small groups of the couple posed with their respective parents and close families. A group of everyone present may also prove worthwhile.
As with wedding celebrations a simple cake-cutting picture should be included followed by one featuring the couple raising their glasses as a toast.

Coming-of-age parties

This used to be the twenty-first birthday celebration but in the UK the age of majority has been lowered to eighteen and parties are still

frequently held to celebrate a teenager's coming-of-age.
Coverage is much the same as for any other special occasion and includes portrait studies of the birthday person, groups showing the parents and family and others with the subject's friends. Sometimes the celebrations coincide with the engagement of the person and it is therefore not uncommon for joint celebrations to be held. In cases such as this then the birthday person with his or her partner should be featured in a selection of poses.
Cake-cutting and toasting pictures can also be included, perhaps with the parents looking on.

Hen parties, showers and stag parties

Frequently couples arrange their own individual parties prior to their wedding day to celebrate their last days of freedom.
The male party is known as a 'stag', the female version, a 'hen gathering' or 'shower'. The occasions quite frequently involve little more than a 'crawl' around the neighbourhood bars in order to consume as much alcohol as possible but occasionally more formal celebrations are held in a suitable place such as a restaurant.
The men traditionally hold their celebrations separate from the women and vice versa. Therefore the occasions are restricted to prevent any males from attending the female gathering or females from going to the male equivalent.
A camera taken along captures some unique insights into the behaviour of one or other of the bridal couple. Sometimes, however, it is possible to take photographs that will not be viewed favourably so be careful. Such 'compositions' are likely to show unguarded moments created by intoxication. But, although it is unlikely that any professional coverage would be required, it is not unknown for friends of the couple to take a camera along. An amusing series of candid photographs can be taken of the drinking, joking and eating that is likely to take place on one of these gatherings.
On occasions, the friends of the bride and groom may dress one or other of the couple up in fancy dress (such as baby clothes) or deck them in paper streamers or ticker-tape. This moment should be photographed because it could form an interesting addition to the couple's wedding album.

Children's parties

These are not always easy to handle because children are usually in high spirits at parties. You should try to set up a group photograph of all the children attending the party at the start of the occasion. The remainder of the time you can concentrate on candid studies of the children enjoying themselves whilst they eat, play and take part in games. Often an entertainer is hired to provide conjuring, juggling or similar acts. Your camera can be turned on the children while they are engrossed to capture their expressions. The experience can prove quite rewarding.

Fancy dress parties are also common, especially around Christmas time. All the children should be photographed separately in their fancy dress and a group of winners, if judging takes place, should also be staged.

Parents usually love to buy photographs of their children particularly if there is a certain event or personality involved. At Christmas, take a shot of each child on the knee of Santa Claus; this will be extremely attractive and colourful.

Do not forget, when covering children's birthday parties, to include a shot or two of the child blowing out the candles on his or her birthday cake.

As you need to operate fast and also include a certain amount of action shots taken during the playing of games, an SLR can prove the ideal camera for the job. A fast recycling flash can be used or you may prefer to shoot by natural light using fast films – the location and time of day will determine which method is best.

House parties

Celebrations held in private homes are seldom easy to photograph. There rarely seems to be enough room to manoeuvre between the guests and setting up posed shots is often out of the question. If the party has been thrown for any particular reason, then you should aim to concentrate on that reason. Obviously, if it is a birthday party then you should locate the birthday person to take a couple of portraits.

There is little else to do other than to concentrate on taking candid

pictures of the guests enjoying themselves. Small groups of people engaged in conversation are sometimes worthwhile.
From a commercial point of view, such events are generally a disaster. Most professional photographers turn down these occasions because they are rarely profitable and the photographer is often 'badgered' by people wanting to be photographed but unwilling to buy the resulting studies. However, such occasions can present a different challenge to a keen amateur. The pictures can be highly appreciated, and may pay for themselves with a few sales.

Wedding anniversaries

These are frequently held in small halls or private homes. Once more such affairs tend to be relatively informal and the photographer finds it difficult to obtain any orderly shots. If the occasion is a special landmark such as a silver (25 yrs) or golden (50 yrs) wedding anniversary then the celebrations may be better organized.
Besides producing photographs of the happy couple, you should also do small groups of people such as parents with the couple, brothers and sisters with the couple and not forgetting the children of the couple. If there is a cake then take a cake-cutting picture followed by a toasting shot.
The rules are the same for any of the above celebrations; work quickly and try to capture to happy smiling expressions. A fast recycling electronic flashgun is a must, because many of these celebrations are staged indoors and at night. Sometimes fast films and wide aperture lenses can be used when the ambient light is relatively plentiful.
As already mentioned, a 35 mm SLR camera is a good tool for the job and although there is some loss in quality on big enlargements, a small compact camera does provide greater versatility especially when working in small rooms.

Formal gatherings

There is much greater professional involvement with formal dinners, dances and parties. Many banquet suites have arrangements with

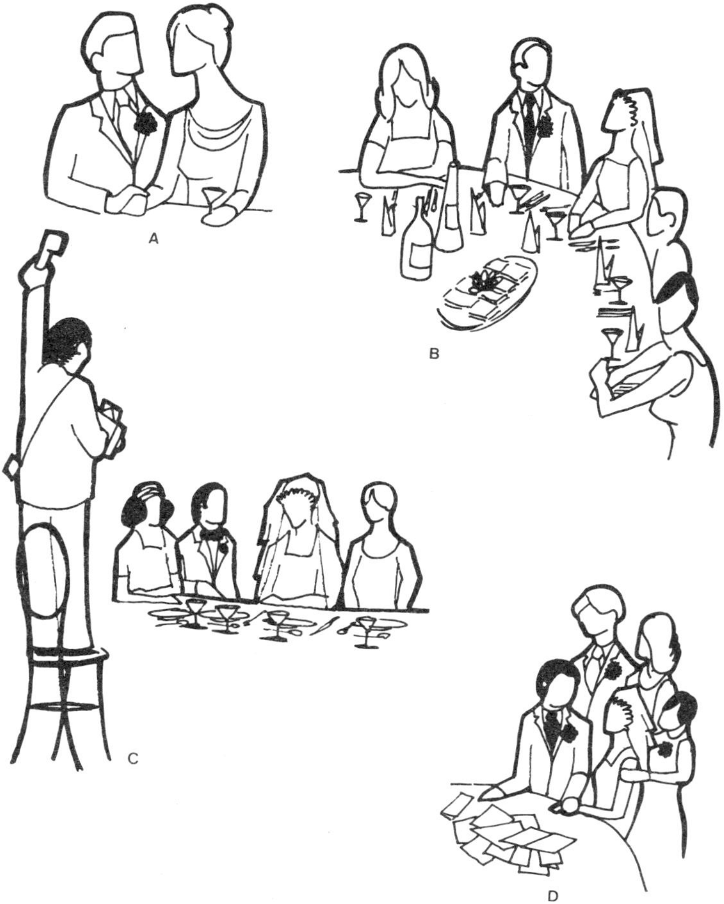

Dinners and dances. A. Table shots can be taken as individual couples or as groups. A wide-angle lens is often required but make sure your flash covers the angle of view. B. A high viewpoint is often necessary and a chair or step-ladder is ideal for this purpose. C. Electronic flash should be taken off the camera and held high to avoid stark lighting and possible 'red eye' effects. D. Groups may look tidier if you stand some of your subjects behind those seated.

particular firms of photographers. This often means that other photographers are not permitted to take pictures on the premises. In view of this, if you wish to take photographs at a function held in a private suite, you should check out the position before booking the job. The situation can become unpleasant if you set up ready for action and are confronted by the suite's official photographer eager to assert his rights.

Formal occasions are very demanding on the photographer, more so than most people think. Today there is a high level of professionalism and competition can be fierce when it comes to securing contracts. Unless specifically requested to attend for the purpose of taking a few photographs for non-commercial ends, if you are purely amateur you are best advised to forget the idea of freelancing at functions. There are a number of firms specializing in banquet and dinner photography and these advertise for extra personnel from time to time in the photographic trade press. Amateurs wanting to do this type of photography can become quite successful by joining one of these firms.

The pace of a dinner/dance is rapid, the guests are sometimes rude, can be blunt and very uncooperative. The reason is because many people regularly attend dinners arranged by clubs or social organizations. Every time they attend a function, which may be several times a month, they are confronted by a photographer. Naturally they become tired of posing for the the same familiar shots, often in front of the same photographer. Nevertheless, there are photographers who revel in these occasions and some of them profit considerably.

The technique for covering dinners and dances is to pick a suitable spot near the entrance of the suite. A toastmaster normally marshals proceedings and announces each couple as they arrive. If you stand near him, as each couple enters you are well-placed to receive them. If they are cooperative then you can take them aside for your photographs.

It is best to take full-length studies because women are generally proud of their dresses and like to be photographed when they are looking their best. A hand-held camera and electronic flash are essential and 6 × 6 cm equipment is commonly the best-suited format. This is because a well-tested system of operation is frequently connected with dinner/dance coverage. Processing and printing is usually completed within a couple of hours of taking the photographs so that they can be returned and sold at the function later in the evening. Roll film proves easier to handle for laboratory staff involved with fast turn-round times.

Another way of covering formal dinners is to provide instant pictures by using a Polaroid based camera. Some photographes operate enterprising systems whereby they work with a colleague supplying key fobs containing photographs. The operator takes the photographs, often using a camera that exposes four small frames on a single sheet of film. This is done by revolving a turret style lens to expose a quarter of the film area in turn. The second operator takes the exposed film, cuts it and mounts the individual photographs in key fobs and returns to the tables and sells them to the customers.

This method of covering dinners is often worked in restaurants and social clubs where a large number of people may gather. It takes a surprisingly short time for a pair of quick operators to complete their work and thus be on their way to the next assignment. The one drawback is that the instant cameras capable of producing the four exposures are initially expensive to buy. Once purchased however, they can be profitable.

When covering formal occasions with a roll film camera, fast action and quick focusing may cause your judgement to be slightly out. By opting for a small aperture, say *f*8, you will have a margin for any slight focusing error that may occur. Low light levels inside some halls also make focusing awkward.

You are most likely to be working with flash. Computerized guns are very helpful because they take care of the exposure problems for you. However, you need to master flash technique so that your results are technically good. The flash-head should be kept away from the lens axis in order to avoid 'red eyes'. If you have the space available, find a suitable background and position your subjects a few feet in front of it. A flash head held fairly high directly above the camera position minimizes any shadows characteristic of direct use of flash. If you are working at a location that has a low and light coloured ceiling, then you may be able to use bounced flash which, in many cases, proves to be more flattering.

Some people prefer full-length studies especially if they have dressed up for a formal function. It is wise to ask your subjects whether they favour a close-up portrait or a full-length study. With close-ups showing a man and his wife or lady friend; keeping the heads close, perhaps with the man's arm around the lady's waist, allows for a tight composition.

Those specializing in banquet coverage normally have a good system operating. The photographer leaves as the guests sit down to their dinner, hands his films into the laboratory for urgent processing and printing and then may return to take table shots for which orders are taken and sent on later. A second person returns to the suite a couple of hours later armed with the results of the photographer's earlier work and proceeds to sell them.

Table shots are not always easy. The best way is to place couples at one end of a table, the men standing behind the ladies forming a tidy group. However this is seldom possible because you are required to take the shots while the meal is in progress. A high vantage point is often called for and a chair usually suffices. A moderate wide angle lens (about a 55 mm on a 6 × 6 cm square format camera) is useful but even then it is not easy to prevent an untidy air about some of your photographs. If you are working with a wide-angle lens ensure that your flash has a wide enough area of coverage to prevent the edges from being blacked out.

Annual dinner/dances, such as those run by sports clubs, or companies are often much easier to cover than the more frequent Rotary and Masonic functions. This is chiefly because employees may not be regular dinner-goers.

It is also possible to secure a fee from a company to cover your operating expenses whereas at the majority of formal functions you are expected to work entirely on speculation, a hit-and-miss affair if you are working with a particularly difficult group of people.

Company dinners are sometimes formal but, depending on the status of staff attending, can be very informal. They may prefer a discotheque to the formal band. You are likely to find that more guests are cooperative, the job is much easier to cover and rewarding as well. People often like to have photographs taken with their workmates and groups, small and large, are popular.

When most of the guests are employees of the firm it is unnecessary

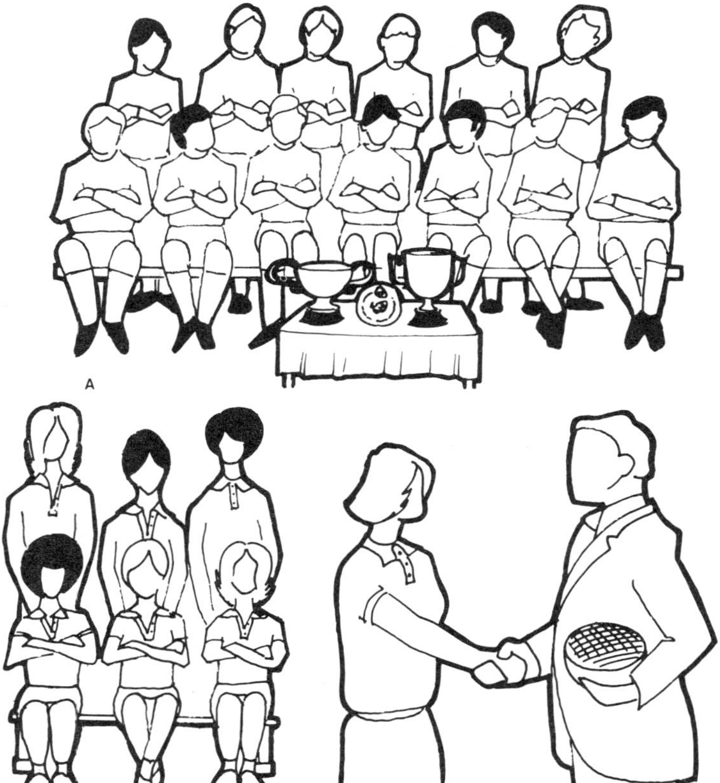

Team groups. A. The front row should be seated or perhaps kneeling and the back row standing. Include trophies, etc. in the foreground and ensure all players have their arms folded. B. Small groups can be taken with everyone standing or with some seated. C. Include the presentation of the trophy.

to present the finished work on the night. Instead a set of small preview prints can be sent to the firm's social organizer so that they can be displayed on a notice board in the company canteen or other suitable place. Orders will then come direct from the firm.
If you are requested to cover a firm's dinner/dance then it is best to obtain an order from the company and to request a full brief if any special photographs are required.

Other company functions

If you work for a large and socially active firm and you own a camera you could make yourself available to those responsible for sports and social organization. There are numerous occasions which require photographic coverage. Some firms have their own in-house photographic units, others use the outside services of professional photographers but there may also be some opportunity for the amateur enthusiast within the employ of the company to take on assignments where professional services are not feasible.
Retirements are obvious events to record photographically, showing the retired person with his colleagues, shaking hands with the company chairman and receiving his gift. Firms, however, seldom think of hiring a photographer.
Public relations exercises are frequently photographed and here there may be the added chance of securing a fee from a newspaper or trade publication if they use one of your photographs. Public relations work can lead in all directions. The firm may be visited by some important dignitaries, even Royalty. Although it is highly likely that the press will be involved there may also be a chance for you to picture the visitors with a group of company directors touring the factory or firm. The company may have become involved with a charity and pictures may be needed as funds are handed over to the particular cause.
Perhaps your company has recently added a new product to an existing range. There are various ways of showing the product and the main sales-orientated photographs will probably be taken by an experienced advertising photographer. However, photographs for press use showing directors or a pretty girl member of staff with the product could be useful. Sometimes this type of photograph is

required on the spur of the moment and the local professional may not be available. It is then that you, as a keen amateur, could temporarily fit the bill.

Conferences, meetings and seminars also provide scope for an aspiring in-house photographer. The delegates and speakers can be taken as portrait studies followed by informal action photographs of them giving demonstrations and speeches. Firms frequently do not want to go to the expense of spending limited budgets on professional photography for these events – but they may pay you a small bonus on top of your expenses for providing a series of record shots.

Even candid studies of your workmates going about their jobs can make very interesting photographs which can earn you extra cash. These can be sold to your friends and may also be required by your firm for company reports and features.

Take care not to allow your sideline to interfere with your working duties, also ensure that you do not break any part of the Official Secrets Act or your own employer's policy if you work in a restricted or official capacity.

Sports occasions

A winning team is always a ready market for photographs. Team groups should be set up carefully, outdoors if the sport is an open air one, inside if the sport is played indoors. It is normal to seat the team captain in the centre of the front row and to build up the other players equally on either side and behind him.

Thus, with a football team it is general for the captain to sit with a ball or trophies before him with the forwards seated on either side of him. The goalkeeper and defenders stand behind.

Today there is more freedom even with sports groups. Formal chaired arrangements are not so widely used and it is quite common for the defence to stand behind the front row who may be squatting on their haunches.

In formal groups try to aim for tidiness and uniformity. Players should fold their arms across their chests or stand with their hands behind them. Make sure that all of them have adopted the same pose.

It is customary for sportsmen to be photographed with the 'tools' of the trade. A rifle club for example should be holding their guns. There is then no mistake about what sort of sport the group are engaged in.

A little imaginative thinking can conjure up some delightful sporting pictures with a difference. For example, if you are covering an archery club, instead of posing them all in the normal way, take them as a line-up. The members can be standing in line with their bows drawn to the full. This way a greater impact is given to an otherwise standard photograph.

Club presentations are not to be missed. Position yourself so that you can photograph the award winners at the exact moment that their prizes are handed over. A word beforehand with the presenter ensures that his and the winners' faces are turned towards the camera at the appropriate moment.

Another interesting way of taking a team group is to have them dressed other than in their sporting clothes. For example, some clubs adopt a standard form of dress off the field and the team may all wear identical suits or blazers. A carefully arranged group dressed formally offers an alternative to the norm.

A novel idea which has been used by certain press sports photographers is to depict amateur teams in their normal working clothes.

For example, a local amateur football team may have had a good run in the Football Association Cup where they have been matched against stronger professional opponents. Rather than show them in the press as a general team group, the amateur sportsmen have been lined up dressed as the butcher, the baker, the scaffolder or whatever and this not only shows that they are amateurs at their sport but also indicates that the team has been selected from people in varied walks of life.

A study of the work of top professional sports photographers is certainly inspiring and can offer some ideas for improving your own shots of the local club.

There are many ways to provide a service as a social photographer. This section of the book only skims the surface. A look around you will present hundreds more possibilities.

Presenting the Results

There is absolutely no point in spending considerable effort taking well-composed and correctly exposed photographs if your end product is ruined by poor printing and presentation.

Presentation is just as important as taking the photograph. A mediocre photograph can look a good deal better by tasteful presentation. A great photograph can look terrible if poorly presented.

If you are doing a job for financial reward then you must ensure that your results at least *look* professional. Poor printing looks cheap and unattractive and will have less chance of acceptance and even fewer chances of repeat commissions.

Some photographers feel that the only way to have good prints produced is to print them themselves. Unfortunately, many professional photographers find that they are kept fully occupied in creating the images on film and therefore the darkroom side must be 'farmed out' to a professional laboratory. It is also likely to be less expensive, if you cost your time, to let the laboratory do the printing.

The main advantage of doing your own colour printing is that you can 'hand print' each negative to the result you desire. 'Hand printing' from a professional laboratory is very expensive, whereas their machine print prices are relatively inexpensive.

Choosing a laboratory

The expansion of colour photography has seen a marked increase in the number of professional processing and printing laboratories. A glimpse through any of the professional photographic journals reveals just a few of them. Most of the top laboratories advertise to some extent. The cost of processing and printing services varies from laboratory to laboratory; so too do the standards. Any photographer using the services of a laboratory for the first time is best advised to shop around for the best prices in combination with an acceptable standard of reliability.

As an amateur, do not be afraid to approach a laboratory offering a professional service. As long as you are not sending in negatives from 110 or 126 cameras, and your films are not just a jumble of hit and miss holiday snaps then the laboratory will accept you as a customer.

Never use the drug store or photodealer style developing and printing services for commercial work or any work of importance. Although some of these places profess to offer a professional standard of service, most certainly do not live up to their claims and the results are dismal. The reason is that such laboratories make their profits on a high volume of work. As most of this work comes from amateurs and snapshooters who are not discerning, the films are lumped together and printed as an average lot. Professional laboratories do not work like this. Each negative is individually printed by trained technicians with a high degree of skill. Colour corrections are made according to the density of the negatives and prints are customized even though the bulk of them may be printed on automated printing machines.

The automation of printing lines has rapidly increased the standards of work turned out by laboratories and has of course improved the turn-round time of customer orders. Early machinery was far from technically brilliant but today it is sometimes difficult to determine whether a print has been hand-produced or machine-made.

The above refers chiefly to colour. Black-and-white prints are still largely produced by hand and again the standards set by the leading laboratories are extremely high.

Answer a few advertisements in the trade journals by requesting brochures and price lists then set about trying a few with some test negatives. Try taking a few exposures of the same subject at exactly the same exposure, have the film processed and send one negative to each of several laboratories. Compare the results when the prints arrive back.

If you find a laboratory that offers a first class service coupled with reliability and at the right price, then stick with them. A good laboratory can be the photographer's best friend and can help turn the occasional poor negative into a saleable item.

Prints and print sizes

Most laboratories in the UK and the USA quote their print sizes in inches. Colour prints more specifically seem to be spoken of as 8 × 10 in, 6 × 8 in, 5 × 7 in, 5 × 5 in, $3\frac{1}{2}$ × 5 in and so on. Black-and-white prints are quite frequently referred to by metric sizes, with for example an 8 × 10 in print being 20 × 25 cm.
Papers come in a wide range of surfaces. Some are best suited to particular types of work with the silk and lustre surfaces of both colour and black-and-white papers being generally better suited for social photography. The gloss finishes are preferred for commercial and industrial subjects.

Proofing and preview prints

In the UK it is standard practice for social photographers to fly around like lunatics, despatching exposed films to laboratories for urgent processing and printing, and to take back 'proofs' to weddings and other events the same day. Same day 'run-backs' are not common in the USA particularly because photographers spend more time covering receptions than their UK counterparts. There are mixed views about the value of this exercise and many believe that the demand for same day previews is on the decline. The idea was that a set of rough proof prints would be taken along to the wedding to secure the orders of the guests and the newly married couple. A few years ago this seemed to work extremely well and almost everyone wishing to order did so on the day. Nowadays, some guests do order the same day but the couple and their family are more and more often asking for a few weeks in which to choose their orders.
If, however, a family is gathered from far and wide it is of course far easier for them to order prints on the day of the wedding than at some time in the future. By the same token if a proof-back system has not been in operation in a particular area and you suddenly start doing it, then the novelty value alone may bring in the desired orders.
Some laboratories offer a same-day proofing service to wedding

operators and you are best advised to check with the individual laboratories for information on this.

What is a proof and what is a preview print? Well, different photographers have their own names for the type of prints they offer, but it is generally agreed that *proofs* are rush prints which have been produced completely void of any corrections and shading. *Preview prints* are finished prints that have been produced by a laboratory as a 'package' deal without proofs being previously supplied. These same preview prints are probably placed in a numbered proofing book (the page numbers correspond with the number of the print) and are shown to the couple as proofs would be, for the chief purpose of obtaining orders. Once orders have been placed the previews in the book can be removed and placed in mounts and albums. The system thus alleviates the cost of preparing rough proofs in the first place.

There are differing ways of selling your wares at a reception. One method is to place the proofs in clearly numbered pages in a proofing book and this is shown around. The customers quote the numbers of the prints they require and these are written in a duplicated receipt book under the customer's name. Payment is made at the time of ordering, the only sensible way to work. If customers want to pay on receipt of the prints then there is always a problem obtaining the money at a later date.

Other photographers prefer to stick their photographs up on a board so that a greater number of people can view them at one time. A further method is to leave them loose on a table for people to browse through. The latter system can be difficult because people tend to pick prints up and walk off to show others. In the end there is a strong chance of losing half of your prints and therefore this method of operation is not recommended.

Presenting the results

Today photographic mounts and albums are expensive. However the cost should be passed on to the customer. Nobody minds paying a little extra for something providing the product is better as a result. *Never* supply loose prints to a wedding or social customer unless they are specifically requested. Prints should be neatly spotted and placed in clean well-styled folders or mounted in albums or frames. Many photographers avoid the cut corner style of mounts because they look untidy and cheap. The slip-in style is preferable because the customer can always take the print out if they want to. The paste-on variety of mounts are also rather pleasant but the prints cannot be removed from them without the risk of damage.

Again, the major suppliers advertise in the professional photographic press and there are also numerous wholesalers who will readily supply professional wedding and portrait products to the serious amateur market.

White mounts generally look best for monochrome prints, chocolate brown, maroon, grey or dark green look best for presenting colour photographs. Most mounts are blocked with an attractive pattern in one corner of the cover and the print area is generally bordered in gold or a similarly tasteful colour.

The reverse of mounts can be printed in one corner with your name, address and telephone number or you can use small, self-adhesive printed labels which can be obtained quite cheaply. If your work is good then it is your biggest and most flattering form of advertising. Your name and address on the back ensures that you may be contacted by anyone who may wish to hire you. Personal recommendation is one of the keys to success. When much of your work comes through the channels of recommendation then you know that you are on the path to success.

Retouching of prints

Never allow your prints to be released with dust and scratch marks on the surfaces. By using a professional laboratory you should ensure that any marks on prints are minimal. If there are noticeable blemishes and marks, such as hair marks on your prints then most emphatically do not accept them. Return them to the laboratory and demand a new set of spotless prints.

Minor dust spots, providing they are few in number can be easily spotted out using water colour paint or special retouching inks or dyes available from photographic suppliers.

The way to do this is to keep a fine sable hair brush as dry as possible and to just dab little tiny spots of paint (or dye) onto the area of the print in need of attention. This is often known as 'spotting' the print.

Take care not to overdo things or the spotting will show. Also be careful about wetting machine-made colour prints because this can remove the surface of the paper and make unsightly marks which ruin the print.

Mounting and framing

The techniques of mounting and framing are beyond the general scope of this book because they can become specialized arts of their own. However, most photographers should be capable of simple mounting operations.

Albums can be obtained with either slip-in or paste-on leaves. The slip-in variety are obviously the easier choice but mounting into card leaves is not difficult.

Dry mounting tissue can be used. Sheets of this are placed on the print backs, trimmed to fit the size of the print. The corners are then heated with a special iron to make them tacky and the print is placed in position. The surface of the print is then heated so that the remainder of the tissue reacts thus bonding it to the leaf. You must take care not too overheat the prints – check the manufacturer's instructions for dry mounting.

Aerosol adhesives are now available that do the same job. They tend to be a bit messy but a quick spray onto the print back and leaving the print for about 30 seconds secures a permanent bond with the leaf when it is stuck down.

More elaborate methods of mounting involve the use of an expensive dry mounting press but this allows for canvas mounting and heat sealing to become more readily possible.

Simple frames can be made by anyone capable of using a saw and mitre box (for making the corner cuts accurate). Other than that several manufacturers offer ranges of attractive ready-made frames with or without glass.

Pricing

Knowing what to charge for your services is always difficult to determine, especially when you are just starting your own business. The construction of your price scale is dependent on numerous factors, most of which are described below.

In addition to covering your overheads, you need to determine what your time spent on a job is worth per hour. This means that your total charge will consist of overheads, material costs, and a charge for the number of hours involved.

Competition

The competition, or lack of it, within your area has a natural bearing on prices. You should not be forced into a position of structuring your prices simply to suit your opposition. Obviously, if you are wildly more expensive than a competitor while your service is similar, then you could lose out. Similarly, low prices can turn customers away because they may feel the product you are offering is of poor quality.

You should carry out extensive research into your opposition. You need to be aware of what they are charging; but, of greater importance, you should be conversant with the type of services they provide in comparison to your own.

Price cutting exists in photography just as it does elsewhere in the free market. However, reducing prices just to attract business away from your competitors rarely pays off and many photographers have gone out of business as a result of such tactics. Set your prices in line with your services from the start and ensure that your standards are high. Your prices should reflect the type of work that you are doing.

You should not attempt to handle your own bookings until you are absolutely convinced that you are capable of running a professional-style enterprise. It does not matter how many hours you spend at photography, nor does it matter whether or not you work elsewhere during the week. What does count is your attitude and the way you operate your business. It is not good for the photography business, nor for the customer, when amateurs set up simply and purely to undercut their professional colleagues. Doing a job on 'the cheap' in this way must be deplored because you will be doing nobody any favours, particularly yourself.

If you want to win friends, from the start apply professional thinking to your activities and then you will have a greater chance of success.

Area

The place where you work also has a bearing on the prices you charge. If you are fortunate enough to have business premises then you need to consider your overheads. Items such as rent, rates and electricity are all legitimate overheads that must be covered by your income. Similarly, a proportion of your household overheads apply if you use your home as a base.

Naturally, if you operate from stylish premises in a wealthy area then your overheads are higher. In view of this, you will probably price your work higher to compensate.

The competition existing in your area also affects the prices you can expect to charge. An abundance of competition often tends to keep prices down in photography, as in any other business. London, for example, supports a wealth of photographers, yet you will find that the prices charged by wedding photographers may be substantially less than in a rural area.

Photographers working in places where unemployment is high find that this results in less demand for their work. Many photographers who are affected by low sales because of regional characteristics, charge an operating fee to cover their initial expenses on each job. This may not apply to photographers who enjoy the profits from high print sales.

It is important to remember that photographs are still a luxury item, and to this extent people can go without them if they cannot really afford them. Experience alone will prove to you the best methods to work in your own area. You should not be afraid to try different methods of working until you arrive at the best system to suit your own operation.

Package deals

Many photographers take advantage of 'package' deals provided by many professional colour laboratories. Such systems involve the laboratory processing and printing, to finished print standards, each negative on your film. The prices charged for the service is normally a reduction on the cost of normal reprints.
Buying your laboratory prints in this way enables you to know your expenditure on a job before you embark on it. You are able to work out what to charge your customer for each print depending on the cost of your package deal and other overheads.
But, perhaps the simplest way of selling your work to the customer if you are buying your prints under this scheme, is to sell *them* a package. Many photographers work this sytem. They have each roll of film taken processed and printed as a package by their laboratory. They then offer a number of prints in an album for a pre-fixed price. The advantage is that you know what you are going to earn before commencing your assignment. Any re-orders are an added bonus and can be printed from the negatives which are numbered to correspond with the prints in the bride and groom's album.
In order to get to grips with this method of marketing your work, the following example should explain it more clearly.
This example is based upon you shooting three rolls of 120 film, twelve on; 36 prints in all.

Your overheads for covering the job:

3 rolls colour negative film		£ 4.00
Travel to and from wedding		£ 3.00
Package deal at laboratory		£21.00
Album and leaves		£11.00
	Total outlay	£39.00

On top of this you should add what you feel your time is worth for, let us say, three hours work. Let us assume that your time is worth £7.00 per hour. Add this to your expenses and you have a figure of £60.00. You now have to add to this a percentage for overheads and a business profit. You might end up with a package price of £90 to the bride and groom for an album containing 30 photographs. Additionally, you must include the cost of mounts for any extra prints that are not included in the album.

Reprints will cost about £1.00 for each 6 × 8 in. On top of this you may have to buy mounts. These may cost you 30p each for quality products. So, your overheads for each additional print ordered is already £1.30. You must allow for your time and office overheads and a profit margin of at least *100%* should be achieved. You may decide to charge £3.00 each for your prints.

With the above in mind, you can determine how much you will charge your customer for an album containing a number of prints. Assume that you are providing an album containing 20 prints. Allowing a *100%* mark-up on the cost of the album and leaves brings the price of this to £22.00 plus the resale price of 20 prints adds a further £60.00. It is normal for photographers to charge a little less for the 'package' deals and therefore instead of pricing it at £82.00 you might feel that £75.00 is a more attractive price. Remember that these figures can only be regarded as guidelines. Do not forget to add state taxes or (in the case of the UK) Value Added Tax to the prices that you will be paying your suppliers. Similarly, do not forget that the taxman requires his share of your profits and accounts must be kept for his purpose. In the UK you do not have to register for Value Added Tax unless your income reaches a certain amount. However, you are best advised to check out the exact tax position as it applies to you.

Minimum order requirements

Not all photographers work to a package deal system either when dealing with their laboratories or with their customers.

Some may charge a fixed fee to attend and cover the job, thereafter charging a set price for every photograph ordered. Others do not charge a fee and derive their entire earnings from the profits to be made on print and album sales. In such cases it is very common for photographers to enforce a minimum order requirement.

This means that the customer must agree to spend a predetermined amount on buying the photographs. The actual amount naturally varies from photographer to photographer, but it is normally sufficient to ensure that there is no loss of expenses and allows some profit margin as well.

It is difficult to advise on what sort of basis to operate this system. You obviously need to ensure that you do not lose money. You could enforce a system your customers must order an album containing a set number of prints. You may want to take this further so that your customers guarantee to buy a fixed number of photographs in addition to an album. The system can be varied to suit your own preferences.

People are somewhat adverse to being 'told' what they must spend. Because of this the minimum order method of working has certain disadvantages. It may cause doubts about the ability of the photographer. The argument being that a photographer need not take as much care about his work if he is guaranteed a fixed income before he picks up his camera. If his work is based more on speculation then he is encouraged to work harder to ensure that people will want to buy his prints because of their quality; which brings me to the next method.

Offering work on speculation

At the time of booking, the customer pays a deposit and nothing else. This shows good faith and ensures to some extent that they are not going to go out next day and book someone else. From there on they are not committed to buy anything. Your success depends completely on your ability to turn out good photographs and upon the public's desire to want to buy them from you. In theory the photographer could be in a precarious position. You may cover a wedding, pay all of your suppliers and then turn up with your set of photographs only to find that nobody wants to buy them. After the event there is absolutely nothing you can do about it. You have

agreed to operate this system and if the customer does not wish to order your prints then that is all there is to the matter. However, in reality, this seldom happens.
The method proves that the photographer must have confidence in his ability. On the psychological side, the photographer operating this type of system strives to achieve better results and this is probably one reason why the system works so well. It is also a good selling point. People calling at your door have nothing to pay, apart from a small, returnable, goodwill deposit.

Photographers operating on a speculation basis, and there are a good many, normally use the services of a colour laboratory which offers a free proofing service. The system is simple and works extremely well. The photographer takes in his films after the wedding and the laboratory provides a set of proofs to take back to the wedding, free of charge. The laboratory, of course, holds onto the negatives to ensure that they receive the finished print orders; the cost of producing the free proofs is absorbed in this way.

Fee charging method

There are a growing number of photographers turning towards this method of working. Many believe it is more professional to charge an operating fee in these days of steeply rising prices. After all, if you went to see a solicitor or an accountant, you would expect to pay him for his services. For some reason, photographers have always been expected to cover social occasions for nothing; depending on the willingness of the public to buy the pictures they take. Slowly things are changing. Photographers, when they are earning their livings from their work, are professionals like those involved in other fields, yet, they are not always treated as such.
If you were taking editorial or advertising photographs, then you would expect to charge a fee for your time and to cover your overheads. Why then do some photographers refuse to charge a fee when covering a wedding?
It is of course up to you to select the best of method of working to suit your own ideas of what you want to earn.
One method is to charge the fee at the time of booking along with a

deposit which is deducted from the cost of the couple's orders. Further to these initial payments, you could then offer your prints for sale on a speculative basis.
Other photographers charge a fee as well as imposing a minimum order requirement, or a fee additional to offering a mandatory package deal. Different systems work according to competition in your locality, the service you provide and according to your success in attracting business.
There are no hard and fast rules which can apply to the operating of a particular system. What may work well for one photographer may not work at all for you. So, in the first place, you need to take a clear view of each of the methods outlined and put the one you think is best suited to your individual requirements into operation. If you find it does not bring the desired rewards, then you should not hesitate in changing to a different method.

Other systems

For simplicity, many photographers offer only one print size for sale at social occasions. Others find that it is more profitable to provide a wide choice of sizes. The latter method seems to apply more widely in the USA than in the UK, but marketing methods concerning social functions differ in the two countries.
For example, wedding customers pre-book their services more in the USA than in the UK. This involves the couple going to see the photographer and discussing in fine detail exactly what photographs they would like taken. In addition, many photographers make a rule of 'selling' their finished services in advance. It is not unusual for the couple to order their album, the number of prints to go in it, and pre-book even the prints which will be going into their parents' albums. In the UK this advance planning is almost unheard of.
By the same token, it is not usual for photographers to rush back to wedding receptions with proofs in the USA. In the UK, this method is used chiefly in large cities to take proofs back when it is practical to do so. This means that the couple, their parents and relatives can place their orders on the day of the wedding rather than in advance.
Payment methods also differ between the two countries. In the USA

many photographers stipulate that payments are made in advance of the wedding, often by instalments. By the time the photographer performs his task he already has been paid for the albums and prints pre-ordered by his clients. The UK method usually involves payment at the time when the couple order their photographs. This invariably is *after* the photographs have been taken.

But, to go back to print sizes. The locality tends to dictate what sizes are offered for sale. For example, some photographers have found that the south of England favours 6 × 8 in prints, the north of England favours smaller sizes, 5 × 5 in, and Northern Ireland largely opts for bigger 8 × 10 in prints.

These regional peculiarities may be derived from differences in customer incomes, but it is difficult to say for certain. A photographer in Carlisle, in the far north of England, said that he found it impossible to sell large prints and he believed it was because people could not afford them, even though there was only a marginal difference in price between 5 × 5 in and 5 × 7 in prints. This leads into the discussion of what selection of print sizes to offer.

Dealing in one size prints obviously saves you considerable time and paperwork. Also, if you offer many sizes then you need to be well organized to avoid any ordering errors. It is the view of many that if a customer is shown small prints then he usually orders small prints. Many photographers offer nothing smaller that 6 × 8 in prints and if they are asked to supply smaller prints they always say that it is not economic to offer anything less in size. You should encourage your customers to think big rather than small and try to persuade them to order prints of a reasonable size.

Some photographers provide a wide range of services, especially if they offer package deals. It is not uncommon for some studios to offer a variety of packages at varied prices according to the size of the prints that are ordered. Readily offering varied size prints often leads to a complicated system. While this may be easy to handle once your business is operating satisfactorily, it may bring complications at the beginning. You are well advised to consider offering only one size prints, or, at least, a minimum size. Larger prints can always be offered as extras with frames, etc., to provide a wider service.

Once you have decided on the size of prints which you will be offering ensure that you show your customers proofs or preview prints of the same size when taking their orders. Some photographers, for the reason of economy, show smaller prints than those represented by the finished prints. As stated before, this simply encourages the customer to order small prints. Shown large prints, they will want to order large prints.

If you really feel that you want to offer a variety of sizes, then, for the sake of profits, you should attempt to construct your price list so that the smaller prints are only marginally less in price than the size you are really intent on selling.

This theory is irrespective of your own overheads when buying the prints from the laboratory. If, for example, you want to sell 6 × 8 in prints, but also offer prints that are 4 × 5 in, then fix your price for 6 × 8 in prints and offer the smaller ones minimally cheaper rather than considerably so. This automatically guides most people to buying the larger sizes.

Never be afraid to experiment with your marketing systems, but do ensure that you clearly word your price lists so that your customers are not confused about what services you are offering and at what price. Keep your system simple and you will find it easier to handle.

Pricing for other occasions

The previous sections have applied chiefly to pricing your services for covering weddings, but similar principles apply when costing for other assignments.

Customers frequently want you to cover a job for nothing and many photographers would certainly advise against speculative working when handling other social jobs, unless of course there is a guarantee that you will sell a lot of prints. But other occasions often fail to live up to the desired returns.

Some photographers do make very good livings from covering dinners, dances and similar occasions. Usually these people are geared specially to cope with this type of work. The general practitioners are less likely to find this work profitable. Whilst there are photographers willing to provide their services free of charge at such occasions then organizations presenting such functions will continue to want something for nothing.

Exactly how much you charge must depend on the type of job and the length of time you spend there. Perhaps an hourly charge is the best method of calculating your fee. Alternatively, you could do jobs under the 'package' deal method described for weddings. Parties, christenings and other such occasions should also be priced on a package or fee structure because you are unlikely to sell many photographs.

It is also common practice for photographers to raise the costs of their prints for occasions other than weddings. This is partly because you expect to sell less prints than at a wedding, and you are likely to be asked to work evenings and other hours beyond your norm.

Promoting yourself

It does not matter whether you are the best photographer in the world; if you are unable to communicate with your public then you will have very little chance of success.

Promotion is one of the key factors in operating a successful business yet it is astonishing how many photographers fail on this basic point.

It is important to create an image. Such an image needs to reflect the type of work you do and the kind of services you provide. It must also reflect your own character to a considerable degree. It is easy to create an undesirable image. For example, a bad telephone manner can be very damaging. It does not matter if, in every other aspect of your business you make a good impression; if one facet lets you down then every item might as well.

From the start you must ensure that everything about your business is functional, precise and devised to suit the image you want.

This may start with the way you dress when you go out to see customers. If you dress well – not flamboyantly – but tidily and respectably, then this gives a good impression. The same manner of dress also applies to you and your staff whenever you go out on a job. The way you talk and your attitude towards your clients has a great influence on your business.

As already stated, your telephone manner is very important. A pleasant 'good morning' followed by the telephone number or name of your company (name of company is preferable) are indications that the person answering the telephone is interested. A 'smiling' voice gives the same indication to a caller. Make sure that you sound interested in what the caller is about to ask. Never answer the telephone by simply saying 'hello'. This is bad mannered and can do harm to your business.

Your letterheads, business cards and other stationery, must all be stylish but not pretentious. Use soft conservative hues rather than bold brilliant colours. The typefaces you adopt should be used throughout; on cards, letterheads, brochures, etc., so that your customers readily and sub-consciously connect each item with your image.

Never cut corners when handling your business publicity. It pays to do the job properly and this may mean employing a freelance designer to do the job for you. It is initially expensive but in the end, if the job is well done, it reaps rewards.

Printing and publicity are expensive items but you should remember that they are just as important to the well-being of your business as your camera.

Letters must be carefully typed and personally signed. Again, a sloppy secretarial manner is a poor reflection on your business. If you do not think you can type them perfectly yourself, then try and find a secretary who will do the task for you.

Brochures and advertising material must also be carefully composed and printed. Again, a costly procedure but money well spent. If you feel you are unable to write impressive copy, then use the services of someone who can.

Creating your image may sound like an extremely costly venture. To do it properly it is. There are, however, many advantages to be gained by spending both time and money on your public relations exercises. Start with sharpening your telephone manner. Have tidy letterheadings and cards printed. The rest can be added as you have the resources available to spend on them. Remember to pay close attention to the little things. They are easily overlooked by you, but they can and will go a long way to impress a customer. Clients can be won or lost by the first impression.

Attracting customers

There is no certain way of attracting customers to your door once you have started your business.

Advertising your services in local and regional newspapers, on the cinema screens, by leaflet drops and numerous other ways may bring you a small selection of customers, but the costs incurred can be high and the returns may only be minimal. Some photographers attract much of their work by actually knocking on doors. This may involve a completely cold canvass on doorsteps or following up the names and addresses appearing in the engagement columns of newspapers. The whole method is somewhat based on pressurized selling; a technique which does not appeal to everyone.

Your best form of advertising is always your work, presentation and your ability to get along with the people that matter; your customers. Attractive presentation goes a long way and the good image you have nurtured can be greatly influential in bringing in new business. There are of course many aids to promote your business, but before good money is thrown into advertising and publicity ventures you ought to research the market.

You can always attract a certain amount of free publicity by regularly sending news bulletins about your business to local and regional newspapers. If, for example, you win a prize in a photographic competition, or you are about to open up a shop, a well-written piece sent to the editors, perhaps with a photograph, is usually accepted for publishing. This may not immediately draw custom, but free publicity of this kind goes a long way to getting you and your work known.

In the long term, the degree of success you attain can only be measured by what you, yourself, do to promote yourself. Excellent work, attention paid to the finer points of your job and the provision of personal service to your customers, each play a key role in furthering your business. If you fall down on the quality of your work, or if you present a rude or untidy image, then you will certainly lose customers. Start as you mean to go on and the world can become your oyster!

Index